This heartfelt book from K what
it means to live in the ligh   a life
walked with God. A beauti   se eyes
are on us.

The idea for this book was born before Kate suffered the tragic death of
her beloved husband, Trevor. These reflections on God's eternal goodness
and the promise of the beauty and glory of the world to come then came to
fruition through the harsh reality of loss and death. It means that this is a
book that deals honestly with suffering, but also contains within it a lived
knowledge of the hope and promise that God has given to this world in the
reality that we have our true home in him. It is a book that will inspire and
comfort. I commend it to anyone needing to know more of God's love and
hope in their lives.

In more than three decades of ministry among the poor, we have seen
every kind of suffering, grief, and loss under the sun. Daily we weep with
the broken. We also rejoice daily, and the joy is greater than the pain. The
one reason we are able to endure and to worship with genuine gratitude
through every trial is that we know that our eternal home is with God —
and our life in him, even now, is the reward without compare. This is what
we preach to the great and small alike, and we have seen for ourselves that
his beauty is an everlasting promise, able to change every part of life. We
believe firmly that every Christian should learn what it means to live for
eternity, and Kate Patterson's heartfelt meditation on this theme is a gift I
warmly encourage you to explore.

Kate Patterson is a very special person whose love for Jesus Christ shines through so much of what she says and does. Few people are better qualified to write about 'living for eternity'.

NICKY GUMBEL

Holy Trinity Brompton; Founder of The Alpha Course

In the trials and troubles of life there is no greater remedy than to look up to our eternal inheritance in Christ. So I am delighted to recommend this uplifting and well-written book on eternity that is both profoundly biblical and practically helpful. Read it and rejoice!

J.JOHN

Minister, Speaker and Author

Why do we avoid thinking about the big picture of life and death, especially considering the hope we have in Jesus? I am full of admiration for how Kate has walked the difficult path of loss and for how she is sharing that journey with others now. Full of grit, gutsy honesty and gospel-filled-grace, this is a book which will lift your eyes and fill your heart with God's eternal hope.

CATHY MADAVAN

Speaker, Broadcaster and Author

The promise of eternity transforms Kate Patterson's everyday life, changing a monochrome landscape into colour. Sharing her hard-won vision of the eternal in the here-and-now, she invites us to experience God's joy even in the midst of our darkest days. Read this book and be encouraged.

AMY BOUCHER PYE

Writer, Speaker and Retreat Leader

Kate Patterson's book is a virtual visa in our passport to a place so little spoken of in our churches today. How to live our lives in the light of eternity! That's what's so marvellous about this book. Written from a biblical standpoint, Kate takes us one chapter at a time across the biblical landscape of the reality of eternity. You will find no catch phrases here just solid truth and personal testimony and learning. This is a timely book given the fear saturated world we live in today.

EDDIE LYLE

President Open Doors UK & Ireland

This book has been crafted from the story of personal pain and yet brings such hope. A must read for us all as Kate brings hope and light to anyone going through difficult times and focuses our eyes on the greater narrative of eternity.

REVD PREBENDARY MARK MELLUISH
Senior Pastor St Paul's Ealing & St Mellitus Hanwell; Assistant National Leader
New Wine; Non-Executive Director Tearfund

Reading Kate's honest reflections before God shows how she has journeyed through the valley of the shadow and the valley of tears - and come through, not bitter but with faith, hope and love in the Jesus who has life forevermore ready for us. This is an extraordinary book by an extraordinary woman that will bring you closer to an extraordinary Jesus.

SIMON PONSONBY
Theologian and Author

Christians can easily fall into binary positions; living in denial of their earthy circumstances or blind to their eternal inheritance. Kate Patterson masterfully navigates the tension between suffering and hope. She enables the reader to stand with their feet in the clay and their eyes in the clouds. Rich, raw and beautifully crafted, this book is blessed assurance in time of struggle and uncertainty, shining a new light upon the God who became flesh and moved into our neighbourhood.

REV WILL VAN DER HART
Author of The *Power of Belonging*, Director of The Mind and Soul Foundation

Living for Eternity

Thou, O my God, art ever new,
though Thou art the most ancient;
Thou alone art the food for eternity …

Without Thee, eternity would be another name for eternal misery.
In Thee alone have I that which can stay me up for ever …

Thou alone art inexhaustible,
and ever offerest to me something new to know, something new to love …

For eternity I shall ever be a little child
beginning to be taught the rudiments of Thy infinite Divine nature.
For Thou art Thyself … the heaven in which blessed spirits live and
rejoice.

JOHN HENRY NEWMAN[1]

Living for Eternity

Knowing the God of Forever

KATE PATTERSON

Muddy
Pearl

Published in 2020 by
Muddy Pearl, Edinburgh, Scotland.
www.muddypearl.com
books@muddypearl.com

British Library Cataloguing in Publication Data

A catalogue record for this book is available from the British Library

ISBN 978-1-910012-39-0

Cover design by Lindy Martin

Typeset in Minion by Revo Creative Ltd, Carlisle, Cumbria

Printed in Great Britain by Bell & Bain Ltd, Glasgow

Cover image © Shutterstock 1314283397 by suns07butterfly, 700841782 by deckorator

To my wonderful parents, Martin and Cynthia Peppiatt,
who have lived and loved with eternity in mind.

Foreword

Someone who takes on the subject of eternity has to be a courageous person. A brief scan of the titles in a bookshop will tell you there are very few authors who have ventured into this territory. Yet you are holding a book on that subject, written by someone who can be trusted as a good guide, and one who I know has real courage. Kate Patterson has a unique perspective, as she writes only a few years after her husband Trevor's unexpected and sudden death. There is a poignant context and timing to this book – as it was agreed and conceived while Trevor was still alive. The space and time that has passed between then and now give a depth and maturity to all that Kate has to say.

Many years ago, I trained as an engineer, and was fascinated by the mathematical concept of infinity, especially as it relates to time, that is, eternity. I still love thinking about eternity as a concept, but rarely embrace it personally, perhaps because of being so caught up in the day-to-day pressures of the present. And yet when I am brought up short, through loss in my own life, or in the lives of friends or around us in the community, I realize there is so much more to explore in the midst of this life about what lies ahead.

The writer of Ecclesiastes tells us that 'God has put eternity in our hearts.' It is not just a concept to be wrestled with in our minds, but a reality to be discovered and embraced in our hearts. Kate invites us to discover this for ourselves in a beautifully personal, accessible and down-to-earth way. She helps us see that an eternity with God is not something to be feared as unknown, but as a destination that, if acknowledged, completely impacts and changes how we live today in a positive way.

This book will take you on a journey closer to God, as it has with me. It is ideal for people just starting out on the journey of faith and for those who have travelled with Jesus for many years. Treat this book as a travel guide, absorbing the scriptures and the stories and reflecting on the helpful questions at the end of each chapter, and it will serve you well. Kate writes a telling phrase near the end of the book, when you feel you have journeyed so far and received so much, that you have 'barely skimmed the surface'. Just like using a good travel guide for the first time and discovering that your perspective has deepened and widened, and feeling the sense of excitement that there is so much more to discover, I think you might find, as I have, that this is one such guide. May you be blessed as you use it for your journey too!

Ric Thorpe
Islington
August 2020

Held in Eternity by Love

*Now this is eternal life: that they know you, the only true God,
and Jesus Christ, whom you have sent.*

JOHN 17:3

The past few years have been a crash course for me in the importance of living for eternity. Christianity speaks a lot about eternal life, but, like many of us, I tended to live for the short term. In the summer of 2017, I felt increasingly convinced that we miss out if we live as if this life is everything. I began to write on being eternally minded and soon accepted a book contract.

Then, in October 2017, I went away for a short break to Dorset with my husband, Trevor. On the first day, he popped out for a jog. He was an experienced marathon runner, but an hour ticked by and I became increasingly concerned. I drove down the lane to look for him and my heart lurched as I saw a trail of traffic blocking the road and an ambulance at the end of it. When I told the person at the back of the traffic jam that I was out looking for a runner, they hurried me to the front, and I knew from the expression on the face of the paramedic that it was bad news. Trevor had suffered a freak heart attack and he was already dead. The shock was enormous for me, for our sons and for our church.

I believe that it was God's kindness to us that I had begun thinking on living for eternity. For me, it is no coincidence that Trevor's last talk at our church was part of a series that we planned together on being eternally minded, although I had no idea then how much the eternal perspective would help me through the tough days ahead.

My journey of grief was transformed by discovering that the way to live for eternity is by knowing the God of eternity, the One who has carried me through the toughest time in my life.

I parked this book for a while as we began to face our grief, but returned to it because I believe that all of us desperately need an eternal perspective in this time in history, whether we are facing loss or not. What seems secure can quickly be shaken by economic instability, climate change, a global pandemic and seismic cultural shifts. This life is fragile and our click-now, consumer-driven society has no answers. More than ever, we need to know the way to eternal life – we need to know the God of eternity.

Yet, so often, we live heads down, ignoring the long view. How can we keep our eyes on eternity when daily life is all-consuming? This book grew out of my discovery that it changes how I live and grieve and hope and love when I remind myself of the joy ahead. But it gets even better than that – as we will see, eternal life begins now – because we can know the eternal God today – this side of death.

What a joy to discover that nothing about God is temporary! He is our home, now and forever, not just our Father for a moment but for eternity, not just crumbling sand but the Rock that remains, not just my good Shepherd today but forever, not only the One who created me but the Eternal Creator who is constantly working for good in my life and always will be. All that God is, God always is. It is with awe that I have written about knowing the Everlasting God, aware that these are just first steps on the greatest of journeys; his character, his love and his grace are mind-blowingly greater than these pages can contain. This book cannot begin to span the breadth of our infinite God, but above all, I hope that it may spur you on to seek to know God better.

To truly know God is to adore him. What can we do but worship when we see that our little lives are held in eternity by love?

Whatever life holds for you, may you discover the comfort, security and deep joy of knowing the God of forever. That is what sets us for heaven and sets heaven in us.

Acknowledgements

WITH HUGE THANKS

Johnny, Connor and Ben – your loving encouragement kept me going and your insights have been invaluable.

My wonderful praying friends – this book would not be here without you and I reckon I would be in pieces. I am so thankful for our WhatsApp group and for my church, St John's.

Dad, Ali, Lucy and Kate – thank you for giving that precious gift of your time to comment and for digging me out of many holes!

My editor, Stephanie, and graphic designer, Lindy – thank you for making this book beautiful.

Gift of Blessing Trust – to all our supporters and to the Trustees and Patrons, Clare, Tristan, Rosemary, Jo and David, Bishop Ric and Bishop Richard – thank you for freeing me to write and cheering me on. And thank you so much Ric for the kind foreword!

Above all, all thanks to God – Father, Son and Spirit – now and for eternity.

Contents

Introduction

How do you begin to open up the subject of eternity? Much ink has been spilled discussing eternity and I have not attempted to cover all the theological and philosophical disputes. The heart of this book is that everyday life becomes eternal life when we know the eternal God. It is designed to be read prayerfully, with a response at the end of each chapter. You may want to read it in short sections over a week as part of your devotional time with God or you could perhaps read it with a friend or in a small group and discuss the responses together.

The book is divided into two parts:

Part One, 'Eyes on Eternity', is about why it matters that we live with the long view. God has set eternity in our hearts and we are designed to live with our eyes on the glorious future ahead. When we set our lives towards the eternal, we live differently – anticipation of the destination changes the journey! But we discover that living for eternity is not only about the future. Eternal life is found not in a place but in a person – in knowing the ever-present eternal God.

Part Two, 'Knowing the God of Forever', is a series of reflections on the eternal character of God. God wants to reshape the warped pictures that we carry in our hearts and minds of who he is because he longs for us to know him. Here is eternal life. Here is incomparable joy!

PART 1

Eyes on Eternity

Here is an invitation to embark on the most wonderful journey of all – eternal life. How can we possibly live for eternity? Only by knowing the God of forever. Because when it comes to eternity, God is not only the destination, God is the way!

This is eternal life: that they know you, the only true God, and Jesus Christ, whom you have sent.
JOHN 17:3

Chapter 1

Eternity's Song

God has set eternity in the human heart
FROM ECCLESIASTES 3:11[2]

AN ETERNAL MINDSET

One evening a few years ago, Trevor and I were driving to a speaking engagement in Sussex. We were faithfully following the satnav, as it was a little out of the way, but as the country road narrowed to the point that both wing mirrors brushed the overgrown hedgerows, I began to worry that we had taken a wrong turn. Around the next bend, we saw that the potholed lane was heading steeply down towards a ford running dangerously high with muddy water. There was no way that we could drive through it. The meeting I was due to speak at started at 7.30pm. I looked at my phone – it was 7.25. There was no reception. We had no map. I began to get panicky and finally double-checked the postcode that I had given Trevor to put into the satnav. It turns out that just one digit wrong can be a lot of miles in the wrong direction. There was some lively discussion as to who was to blame, but of course, you cannot have an argument when you are about to preach! I did finally get to the meeting, just in time to speak, having discovered that it is worth setting the satnav with care.

If we don't set our internal satnav with care, for eternity with God, we get lost. Every day brings new demands. We hurl ourselves into the whirl of life's distractions. Our social media age says that this instant is what matters and we lose sight of the long view. But if we are not transformed by God's eternal purposes, we conform to the temporary values around us. We end up passively blending into our consumer society, treating the Creator of the galaxies like just another item to stuff into our crammed cupboards.

Why do we struggle to set our lives for eternity? Is it because we have a distorted idea of what awaits us? For many, eternity is no more than a vague promise of pearly gates in the sky. As a child, I thought it sounded worryingly like an over-long church service. Heaven sounded dull. Pictures of chubby cherubs strumming harps on the clouds did nothing for me. Who wants to make that the focus of their life?

What we are offered is infinitely better – God himself is our eternal destination! The Maker of our wild and wonderful universe, of bouncing kangaroos and sculpted desert dunes, of shooting stars and intricate snowflakes, of flame-brushed sunsets and a baby's chuckle, is anything but boring. He is the Creator of music and art and drama and parties. He is the ocean of truth waiting to be explored – all science and philosophy is his. His love is the source of all the richest parts of our lives – laughter and friendships and intimacy. We will want to live for eternity when we grasp that eternal life is all about knowing him.

HOMESICK

When we set our internal satnav to know the eternal God, it brings us home. God is our true home and we will be homesick without him. In Charlie Mackesy's heart-catching book, *The Boy, the Mole, the Fox and the Horse*, there is an exquisitely simple line drawing of three little figures heading along a curving pathway under a natural archway of interlocking trees. The drawing is in black and white but somehow, I imagine them heading to a sunrise. Underneath the picture are these words,

'I think everyone is just trying to get home,' said the Mole.

Deep down, we all want to come home to God. The wonderful truth is that God is our eternal home and that means that we can come home *today*. There is no need to wait till we die.

I still remember my first camp away from family, feeling desperately homesick. Oh, the relief when I saw my dad arrive! He gave me a huge hug, bundled me into the car and brought me home. Today and every day, our heavenly Papa's welcoming bear hug is waiting for us. In Luke 15, Jesus told us this is what God is like: God is like a father who waits at the door, looking every day for his child who has run away. From far off, God comes running to meet you, to throw his arms around you, to bring you home – forever.

From him we come,
in him we are enfolded,
to him we return.

JULIAN OF NORWICH[3]

Many people have told me that when they first gave their lives to Jesus, it was like coming home. CS Lewis pictures this vividly when he describes the remaking of Narnia,

I have come home at last! This is my real country! I belong here. This is the land I have been looking for all my life, though I never knew it til now ... come further up, come further in![4]

God is longing and waiting for us to come home to him. The needle of the compass of our hearts will keep swinging, until we direct our steps homeward bound. As Augustine wrote, our hearts are restless until we find our rest in God.[5]

ARE WE NEARLY THERE YET?

Although we can come home today to our Father God's embrace, Christians often express a longing for their eternal home. When you have a taste of the air that you breathe when you come home to God, you want to breathe it all the time.

When I was a child, we had several summer holidays in Cornwall. The motorway to the South West was yet to be built so we were dragged out of bed at the brutal hour of 5am to beat the holiday traffic leaving London. It seemed endless – that bone-rattling, joint-stiffening journey in a battered old Peugeot with no seatbelts. There were no screens to distract us and we plagued my parents with the incessant wail, 'Are we nearly there yet?'

What about us? Are we nearly there yet?

There is a delicate balance to this answer, which swings between yes and no, now and not yet. When we entrust our lives to Christ, yes, we are instantly welcomed home to God. There is no need to wait until you die to run into the Father's arms. Even when the journey feels achingly long and life is like the back of a bumpy Peugeot, there is deep joy to be found in God. The essence of life forever is knowing the One who is forever and that can begin right now.

However, we are evidently not quite there yet if 'there' is Paradise. The King of kings has not yet returned to set all to rights. War and injustice darken our news bulletins. A pandemic has power to devastate healthy families and economies. If you are not struggling with sadness, someone dear to you probably is. All creation is groaning, out of kilter, longing for the day when Christ returns. Earth has rejected its rightful ruler and instead of righteousness, joy and peace, the rule of the evil prince of this world is all too evident.[*]

* John 14:30.

So why doesn't God act? Surely God could click his fingers, send a lightning flash and impose his reign by force? God chose another way because the King of Love seeks willing guests for the eternal house party. God sent invitation after invitation through the prophets calling his people back to himself until finally his Son brought the invitation by hand.[*] In Christ, God came himself to bring it, so humbly. Now, we have the brief span of our lives to RSVP.

One day, when Christ returns, every knee will bow before him and this world will be renewed, but until that day, we live in the tension between the now and the not yet.[6] Like the people of Israel in the wilderness, we have been freed from slavery but we are still on a desert journey to the Promised Land. Constantly, God reminds us of our eternal destiny; constantly, Satan attempts to clog our ears with noise and fears. What can we do? Those who have gone before us show us the way; they deliberately reminded themselves of where they were heading. Samuel Rutherford, the seventeenth century theologian who suffered greatly for his faith, describes us as being like mistreated immigrants in this life, but then offers blazing hope,

> Our fair morning is at hand, the day-star is near the rising, and we are not many miles from home.[7]

In the relative comfort of the Western world, it is tempting to snuggle down into our cosseted lives, stick our fingers in our ears and avoid talk of eternity because it means facing the reality of death. Perhaps that is why 30 million adults in the UK are yet to make a will. The millenial motto is YOLO, 'You only live once – so make the most of it!' But there is a cry in our hearts that says we have not reached the final destination. We are 'longing for a better country – a heavenly one' and we cannot smother eternity's song.[**]

[*] Matthew 21:35–37.
[**] Hebrews 11:16.

FREED FROM A CONSUMER LIFESTYLE

The recognition that this life is fleeting frees us from the unending, enslaving and exhausting pressure to build a bigger barn or conservatory or career or bank account or social media following. Long ago, King David wrote that we are but a breath and our days are but a fleeting shadow. We are temporary residents, God's tenants not owners; our permanent home is still to come.[*]

That urge to invest in the temporary is an age-old problem. King David's son, Solomon, knew all about the pointless drive to accumulate stuff – he rivalled Bill Gates with a yearly income of 666 talents of gold, worth trillions today, but in the book of Ecclesiastes, he reminds us that we all come from dust and to dust we all return. That makes our manic consumerism empty and meaningless, as rewarding as chasing the wind.[**]

Have you ever tried to catch the wind? We once experienced the drama of a mini tornado in our local park and tried to chase the spiral of leaves that was higher than the towering oak trees. It left us spinning, struggling to stand. Chasing the wind takes you nowhere.

CHASING THE WIND

Why would you chase the wind?
So desperate to please!
Why strive to catch the breeze
when at each swirling gust, another handful of dust
is falling grain by grain beyond your grasp?
If you dare to stop, you'll see
all our paltry towers come smashing, crashing down.

[*] Psalm 144:4, Leviticus 25:23.
[**] Ecclesiastes 1:14.

Could you quieten yourself to listen
to the song of eternity?
The Everlasting God has set it in your heart.
Our flesh will fail but his love endures,
the end of our story is held in trust,
hemmed in by infinity, each thread secured by Christ,
glory rises from the dust.[8]

Why spend our lives chasing the wind? Despite the illusion fostered on our screens and in our glossy magazines, wealth and fame never satisfy. In 2014, Markus Persson, creator of the computer game, Minecraft, sold it for $2.5 billion only to tweet, 'Hanging out in ibiza with a bunch of friends and partying with famous people, able to do whatever I want, and I've never felt more isolated.'[9]

What a gift to discover that there is more to life! Buried in the bleak ground of Ecclesiastes is the brightest of jewels,

He has made everything beautiful in its time. He has also set eternity in the human heart; yet no one can fathom what God has done from beginning to end.

ECCLESIASTES 3:11

ETERNITY IN OUR HEARTS

How can my tiny heart contain eternity? Can I stuff a cloud into an egg cup? Yet somehow, God has set eternity in our hearts. These words are wings to fly on, carrying us to soar high above the confines of our own little lives. They awaken the knowledge in the core of our being that we have an eternal destiny. They explain why the material world cannot fill the void within, why we dream of more. Science may elegantly explain the workings of our universe, but it cannot begin to tell why my parched soul so thirstily drinks in the beauty of an inky sky scattered with stars. Why is my heart stilled by an amber morning mist resting over the fields? Why should I have been enthralled by a lightning storm flashing across foaming waves while unseen gusts buffeted me until I fought to stand? When buildings and busyness are not crowding our lives, the heavens eloquently declare the glory of God.* We have no excuse not to join the eternal song,

> For since the creation of the world God's invisible qualities – his eternal power and divine nature – have been clearly seen, being understood from what has been made, so that people are without excuse.

ROMANS 1:20

If we dare to face the fact of death head on, we know that we are made for more. We may just be dust in the cosmos but somehow this dust has an expectation of eternity. We long to be eternally loved. Of course, to paraphrase CS Lewis, the thirst for the eternal cannot prove that the eternal exists any more than thirst for water proves that water exists, but it is a giant arrow pointing towards it.

> If I find in myself a desire which no experience in this world can satisfy, the most probable explanation is that I was made for another world. If none of my earthly pleasures satisfy it, that does not prove that the universe is a fraud. Probably earthly pleasures were never meant to satisfy it, but only to … suggest the real thing.

Even the best of our blessings are merely pointers of what is to come, and so, as Lewis goes on to say:

> I must keep alive in myself the desire for my true country, which I shall not find till after death; I must never let it get snowed under or turned aside; I must make it the main object of life to press on to that country and to help others to do the same.[10]

Eternity is in our hearts. If we dare listen, our hearts tell us that there is more to life than these days of ours that disappear in a flash, these spluttering candles that burn away to nothingness.

* Psalm 19:1.

Eternity is in our hearts. Travel across the world and every culture has some sense of the divine.

Eternity is in our hearts. If we deny it, we are no more than a random bunch of molecules and all our morals and manners have no firm foundation.

> *Everything is meaningless. All go to the same place; all come from dust, and to dust all return.*

ECCLESIASTES 3:19–20

Eternity is in our hearts. Even kids are hardwired for eternity. In my time as a school chaplain, I saw how death puzzles them. They struggle with why our bodies stop working, asking questions like, 'Can we put sandwiches in Granny's coffin in case she gets hungry?' Death is a stranger to their thinking.

We resist our mortality because eternity is in our hearts. Ageing comes as an unwelcome shock. Yesterday, I was on an exercize treadmill, wired up like a robot, having my heart checked. Inside, I want to be 25, imagining that I will go on forever. No wonder it is said that death is the fear beneath all fears. After all, who wants to imagine their body burning in a crematorium or rotting in the ground, where, as John Donne, rather too vividly, writes, 'the worm shall feed, and feed sweetly upon me'? Without God in the picture, death is petrifying,

> I run to death, and death meets me as fast,
> And all my pleasures are like yesterday,
> I dare not move my dim eyes any way,
> Despair behind, and death before doth cast
> Such terror.[11]

JUDGE AND SAVIOUR

Why should death bring 'such terror' to so many? Is it the prospect of an endless void, or because we fear that death will bring a final reckoning? Unless we are hardened, our consciences twinge painfully when we face our unwelcome tendency to selfish thoughts and acts. We were made in God's image but fail to live up to it. We may look down on others to try and convince ourselves that at least we are better than them, but, as Bishop Handley Moule wrote, even if they stand at the bottom of a mine while you are on the crest of an Alp, 'you are as little able to touch the stars as they.'[12]

The Bible is clear that there will be a final judgment on our lives. John writes,

> Then I saw a great white throne and him who was seated on it. The earth and the heavens fled from his presence, and there was no place for them. And I saw the dead, great and small, standing before the throne, and books were opened. Another book was opened, which is the book of life. The dead were judged according to what they had done as recorded in the books.

REVELATION 20:11–12

It is hard to write about judgment, partly because I am a child of a culture that judges nothing so harshly as being judgmental, but above all, because we care about the eternal destinies of those we love. I used to flick past verses on judgment, drawn instead to the Saviour who commands us not to judge, who welcomes the prostitute and the tax collector and refuses to stone an adulterer. Yet, that same Saviour preached fearlessly about judgment, warning us of the day when all will be called to account.[13] The Bible takes judgment so seriously that the book of Hebrews describes it as an 'elementary' teaching.* The theologian, Tom Wright, calls it a 'vital and non-negotiable Christian belief'.[14]

* Hebrews 6:1–2.

My friend Marie suffered horrifically in the Rwandan genocide. In 1994, close to 800,000 people were slaughtered in Rwanda by Hutu extremists who were targeting the minority Tutsi community due to long standing rivalries. Tragically, Marie's husband was murdered, as was her beloved grandfather who had helped to bring her up, and her brother and sister. In her village alone, sixty-seven people died. Her loss is unimaginable. She describes one harrowing night,

> *'The horrors of the past were laid out around me, literally. I remember sleeping beside people wrapped in binbags; dead bodies. You would try to block them out while you tried to sleep, but they were there, those bodies, and you knew that you might be next. Life is unfair to some. It's unfortunate I have to say that, but it's true. Life is unfair. But one day there will be a judgment day. There has to be, surely, because there can't be any in this world. Not on the earth. But there will be!'*

There will finally be justice – for Marie and for all who are abused, for the slaves, the poor and the hungry. It all matters to God; it will be judged.[15]

> *We must all appear before the judgment seat of Christ, so that each of us may receive what is due us for the things done while in the body, whether good or bad.*

2 CORINTHIANS 5:10

It is against this dreadful and dark backdrop that the light of the gospel shines with blazing brilliance, revealing that God is both Judge *and* Saviour. We discover that God always planned the rescue operation of the cross. Simon Ponsonby puts it beautifully, 'Judgment is God's final word, but mercy was his first.'[16] When we see the judgment to come, how can we not be filled with wonder that the Judge of all always planned to take all judgment on himself?

> *God did not send his Son into the world to condemn the world, but to save the world through him.*

JOHN 3:17

In Christ, God went to the cross so that we could be forgiven. Such is God's love for you and for me. God so longed to bring us home that he came to earth to fetch us.

If you are yet to know the incomparable, unbeatable joy of coming home to God, Jesus calls you as he called the very first disciples, saying, 'Follow me', 'Trust in me', 'Make your home with me'. Those first followers left everything to follow the Saviour and we can do the same. On our own, we cannot reach the stars, but the Lord of the galaxies can lift us up into his arms.

RESURRECTION HOPE

God loves us so much that with the gift of his Son, he gives the gift of eternal life. It is indeed a gift. It is not that we have earned it but simply because we are loved with a love that surpasses all others,

> *For God so loved the world that he gave his one and only Son, that whoever believes in him shall not perish but have eternal life.*

JOHN 3:16

Receiving this gift changes how we view death and how we live life. For us, it changed how we grieved. It gave us hope that held us through the hardest moments. When I climbed the steps into that ambulance to sit beside Trevor's body, I remembered how Trevor had told me that when he had visited people who were dying and prayed with them in their final hours, he had always known that only an empty shell remained after the moment of death. In that traumatic moment, I was reassured that Trevor himself was no longer there, that he was with God. Trevor's heart may have failed but he is alive because Jesus promises us,

> *'I am the resurrection and the life. Whoever believes in me, though he die, yet shall he live,'*

JOHN 11:25 (ESV)

Did that assurance remove all our sorrow? We have still grieved deeply but found unexpected joy in our tears. Grief is changed when we know that we are not heading for a dead end. We have the hope of eternity with God. Paul's words have rung true for us, we 'may not grieve as others do who have no hope.'* We grieve with hope – that God will tenderly wipe away every tear and that all will be made new. We grieve with hope because as Thomas Moore wrote long ago, 'earth has no sorrow that heaven cannot heal.'[17]

Without the hope of eternity, death is a fierce enemy. Our days pass like a puff of steam from a kettle, a soon-forgotten sentence in the epic story of history. I have no idea of my great grandparents' names. The pages of life turn so fast.

For many of us, it feels as if the pages turn too quickly but there is great comfort that the story is not finished. The end belongs to God. Jesus Christ left the grave empty and death is defeated. The finale is not oblivion. There is no need to drown out eternity's song because we have the wonder of forever with the One who loves us with an everlasting love.

> *Therefore my heart is glad and my tongue rejoices;*
>   *my body also will rest secure,*
> *because you will not abandon me to the realm of the dead,*
>   *nor will you let your faithful one see decay.*
> *You make known to me the path of life;*
>   *you will fill me with joy in your presence,*
>   *with eternal pleasures at your right hand.*

PSALM 16:9–11

---

* 1 Thessalonians 4:13 (ESV).

A PRAYER

Father God, I am full of wonder that you have set eternity in my heart. You made me in your image to live for your glory. I am sorry for the times that I have lived for myself instead of for you, my Maker and Saviour. Today, I put my trust in you, my loving God. Thank you that I can leave my sin and shame at the cross and can come home to you. I praise you that I am forever forgiven and eternally loved.

Amen

If you have prayed that prayer for the first time, please take a look at the Starting the Journey resource page at the end of the book. God is full of joy over you!

TO CONSIDER:

God has set eternity in your heart. Does this resonate, does it ring true with you? Why do you think that might be so?

What is your internal satnav set for? What would it look like to check and reset it for eternity?

Why, and how, do we sometimes try to silence eternity's song?

Can you see yourself running home to God today?

Do you know that you are loved, eternally? Do you believe it? How does this make a difference to your everyday life?

Read Psalm 16:9–11 and thank God that death has lost its sting.

Have I got a decision coming up that would change if I made it in the light of eternity?

Chapter 2

Destination JOY

*Our present sufferings are not worth comparing with the glory
that will be revealed in us.*
ROMANS 8:18

*Our greatest joys are but the firstfruits and the foretaste
of the eternal joy that is coming.*
CORRIE TEN BOOM[18]

Imagine being led to a van with handcuffs on, heading to a ten-year prison sentence, dreading what is ahead. You have been caught by the police for your criminal misdeeds, had your mugshot taken and said your goodbyes. The future is bleak. Now, imagine you are in a taxi heading to a villa on the Mediterranean coast for a holiday with the people you love best in the world. The holiday reading is packed, and you cannot wait to feel the sand under your toes and take your first dip in the sparkling sea. Not long before barbecues on the beach and laughter in the sunshine! And if the Mediterranean coast doesn't excite you, then imagine being on the way to somewhere else, your dream holiday. Already there is celebration in the air as you begin to let the worries of work roll away. The anticipation of the destination transforms the journey. If that is true for a holiday, how much more so when it comes to eternity!

"A new standard of measurement has been introduced
that makes crosses and trials seem light and momentary."

LIVING FOR ETERNITY

Our light and momentary troubles are achieving for us
an eternal weight of glory that far outweighs them all.'
2 Cor. 4. 17

ANTICIPATION OF THE DESTINATION TRANSFORMS
OUR TROUBLES

For the apostle Paul, his eternal destiny put all his troubles into perspective. Despite writing from a Roman prison, he could say that his present troubles did not compare with the glory ahead – the promise of eternity in the presence of our loving God.

It is amazing what people will endure when they feel the goal is worth it. Ballerinas' feet bleed, athletes' muscles scream, and my nephew hurls himself bodily into a bruising, muddy rugby pitch. It took Michelangelo two years to create his sculpture of David, working in the rain, snatching sleep with his boots on, rarely eating. Why do people give themselves like that? In their mind's eye, they see the prize. Within that block of marble, Michelangelo could see his David and so he gave himself fully to bring his vision to life.

As for us, we who follow Christ can endure much when we see the glory ahead. Shortly before Trevor's death, he tweeted these words from Father Raniero Cantalamessa,

'A new standard of measurement has been introduced that makes crosses and trials seem light and momentary.'

I only saw that tweet after Trevor died, at a time when I might have struggled to hear that from anyone else, but it did speak hope to me. There is a new standard of measurement and it is nothing less than the eternal glory of God.

OUTWEIGHING SORROW

Our light and momentary troubles are achieving for us an eternal weight of glory that far outweighs them all.

2 CORINTHIANS 4:17

Have you ever seen those old-fashioned weighing scales which have a bowl on one side and a platform for brass weights on the other side? Imagine those scales weighing the struggles of life on one side against the glory, the wonder of everlasting closeness with God, that awaits. As we yield our troubles to God, the scales tip. Compared to the weight of eternal glory, our troubles are as light as a feather in the wind. God's glory is weighty; the Hebrew word for glory is *kabod* which also means 'weight'. God's presence brings a weight that for Paul made all else seem light. Extraordinary from someone who had been through betrayals and grief, beatings and imprisonment, and who regularly faced the threat of death!

Here is the wonder of wonders – God's glory can outweigh our heaviest, most heart-rending sorrows because God's goodness and his glory are inseparable. That is why when Moses asked to see God's glory, God caused his *goodness* to pass in front of Moses. Moses asked to see God's glory and discovered that God's glory is his character – the God of undiluted goodness in whom justice and love combine – 'the compassionate and gracious God, slow to anger, abounding in love'.* God's glory is weighty with goodness, weighty with outrageous self-giving love.

How can our troubles 'achieve' this weight of glory? Later on, we will think more about how our struggles can be redeemed but here Paul explains it is when, 'we fix our eyes not on what is seen but on what is unseen'.** The scales tip when we look to God. The scales tip when I trust that, compared to his eternal love, the greatest griefs of this moment are exactly that – momentary.

The great heroes of faith through the centuries constantly challenge us to lift our eyes to the eternal view. One of them is Billy Graham whose life had a huge impact on the worldwide church in the last century, adding an estimated three million followers of Christ. One of those new followers was my mum,

* Exodus 33:18 – 34:6.
** 2 Corinthians 4:18.

who was captivated by Christ when Billy preached at Harringay Arena in 1954. She then met my dad at church, so without Billy Graham, where would I be? Together, they went as missionaries to be part of a Kenyan team which planted ten churches during the East African revival and then returned to England to lead St Stephen's, East Twickenham, which in turn has gone on to plant other vibrant churches. My mum was just one of many whose lives were transformed.

Billy Graham always looked ahead. He repeatedly spoke of how our last breath on earth will be our first breath in heaven, encouraging us, 'Knowing we will be with Christ forever far outweighs our burdens today! Keep your eyes on eternity!'[19]

LOOKING FORWARDS

Nothing less than the glory of all God's goodness is ahead, so it is worth looking ahead. Anticipation extends joy! That is why I love planning next year's holidays. To my family's frustration, I often start planning the next one before we leave the holiday that we are on. I scour the internet for deals and buy the maps for our walks. The promise of a break ahead helps keep me going while I wait.

We miss out when we forget that there is glory ahead. Here is joy that fuels our faith – the grave cannot hold us any more than it could hold Jesus! The scary spectre of death cannot terrorize us if we live as resurrection people. We are refugees in this wilderness, Earth, but we have an eternal home. As Augustine says, we cross this desert,

> ... *by a life that is lived in hope*, until we come to the promised land, to the land of the living where God is our portion, to the eternal Jerusalem.[20]

We need hope in order to endure. Hope helped strengthen my friend Marie towards the end of her ordeal, after she had suffered so terribly as a refugee, trekking from camp to camp in fear. She had a dear memory of her brother, describing the beautiful tulips of Holland to her before the war. She had been doing some gardening, planting flowers in front of their house when he stopped and asked what she was doing, and told her what he had learned about the tulips at school.

> 'I can still recall my muddy hands and the sound of his voice as he told me about the tulips. "I can't even dream that in my lifetime I will go to Holland," I said to Evariste.
> "Well, keep listening to the radio – one day they might mention it," he said.'

Long after Evariste and so many others in her family had been killed, she finally made it across the border to Nairobi.

> 'We stayed for a few months with the UN providing food, water and support. For a long time, I didn't know where I was going. Then I was informed that in two days I would be going to Holland.
> "Holland?" I said. I stopped in my tracks. Hadn't my darling brother Evariste told me all about the tulips in Holland? Could it be that this was the same place with the beautiful flowers? I remember telling myself that I could never have imagined I'd be going to Holland. That's why if you believe in God, you know he has a purpose for everything. Of all the countries in the world, why did Evariste mention that one and why did I end up there? God has a wonderful and mysterious plan for each one of us.'

That picture of bright tulips helped sustain Marie through the long and difficult journey to a strange land. Soon after she landed, she saw the tulips dancing in the fields and she knew that picture had been a gift from God.

The joy of our eternal destination can sustain us as it has sustained Christians through the centuries through the hardest times. As we have found, grief and joy can coexist, entwined together. The gold threads of joy shine ever brighter against the dark threads of sadness.

Eddie Lyle is President of Open Doors, a charity working with the persecuted church. He told me that he is often asked to speak on heaven when he visits persecuted Christians around the world. They know what they need to sustain them. The result is an extraordinary joy that often seems lacking in the apparently 'free' Western church. Naser Navard Gol-Tapeh is an Iranian convert to Christianity serving ten years in prison for 'missionary activities'. He wrote from Evin prison, 'I thank God in perfect joy and peace for considering me worthy to be here because of my faith in and witness to Jesus Christ.'[21]

A SOLID HOPE

If God has given us such a hope to live for, why would we ignore it? Have we decided to settle for a comfortable life on earth? Or is it because we have lost sight of the biblical picture and fallen for a Hollywood vision of heaven so wifty-wafty and intangible that it is essentially unreal? As a teenager, I remember watching a dreadfully slushy romantic film called *Heaven Can Wait* which relied far too much on the use of smoke machines to represent heaven as a place where ghostly figures with wings floated about on wispy clouds, wearing white gowns. If that is what is to come, heaven can definitely wait.

The only reason that you would want a ghostly heaven like that is if you made the mistake of thinking that these solid human bodies of ours are somehow intrinsically unholy. But as Charles Williams said, 'The incarnation has forever hallowed the flesh.'[22]

Because the Holy One became flesh and blood like us, we can trust that our bodies can be holy too. When God became one of us in Christ, He gave this physical world a vote of confidence! Even the risen Jesus was solid and real – eating barbecued fish on the beach, inviting Thomas to touch his hands and side. Michael Lloyd suggests that the risen body of Jesus was so substantial that even

Have you ever looked at a scene so beautiful
and tight "Surely there can't be anything more
beautiful than this?"

Marilon sleam in Bavaria - so crystal
clear... well, there is scarcely more beautiful than the
most beautiful scene, most among clearest + while you have

ever expressed...

walls were immaterial by comparison.[23] It was not because Jesus lacked substance that he could pass through walls but because Jesus is the most real thing! That reassures us that God's new creation will be solid and real too.

Life here will not end like an episode of *Star Trek* where we are beamed up to a city in the sky. Instead, Jesus will return to renew all things and heaven will come down! The God who gave Adam and Eve a role in Eden will give us a part to play in his glorious new creation and it will be more fulfilling than any job that you have ever done.

It is this idea of a solid, tangible and wonderful heaven on earth that CS Lewis pictures in many of his stories. There, at the end of all things, the world is renewed and becomes more rather than less real – brighter, richer and stronger. King Caspian takes a sip of the freshwater sea and describes it as 'real' water,

> The King took the bucket in both hands, raised it to his lips, sipped, then drank deeply and raised his head. His face was changed. Not only his eyes but everything about him seemed to be brighter.[24]

The heavenly feast promised in Scripture will not be see-through food. Can you remember the most delicious meal you have ever eaten? The God who invented those tastes will give the best dinner party ever, surpassing any Michelin restaurant with three stars. We will not be less real; we will be able to hug and belly laugh and run and dance. All the best things of this world are only a rehearsal for the next. The fragrances will be sweeter, the water purer and the wine will be vintage. And what about the colours? When I visit Northern Ireland, the rays of the low-hanging sun have a golden quality that makes every shade more vibrant. At times, the green shines out of the grass as if each blade holds a light source. I remember standing on a windswept, glowing evening on the craggy Donegal coast, saying, 'I don't need heaven to be more beautiful than this.' If such beauty is here, what is ahead?

A RENEWED BODY

What about the promise of a new body? Why is it that we so rarely think about this – even in church? Is it because we are unsure what to believe? How could resurrection work if the body has decayed? If the physical brain is the seat of our consciousness, how can we continue to exist when it dies? As if that is a problem for God! It would be child's play for the Maker of our DNA to recreate every intricate spiral without a flaw. The Creator of the atom would not find it hard to combine a handful of them to recreate a brain that carries your individual consciousness. No one knows exactly how our new bodies will be made but the core of who we are is safe with God.

I have always liked the story of the caterpillar who looked up to the butterfly and said, 'You won't catch me up in one of those.' When it comes to envisaging our new bodies, we are like that. If you looked at an acorn and knew no better, would you ever imagine it could become an oak tree? Look at a tulip bulb – is there any clue that it could contain a myriad of colour? How could the dull, woody, grey lump that is a hyacinth bulb burst into a scent that fills my home? Paul tells us that the relationship between our earthly body and our eternal body will be like the difference between a seed and a plant.* Both seed and plant are solid and physical but the second is the fulfilment of the first. Jesus, 'will transform our lowly body to be like his glorious body, by the power that enables him even to subject all things to himself.'**

That is so exciting! Our bodies here are temporary; the future body will be glorious! Jesus promises that we will shine like the sun.*** Our current bodies are like tents but glorious permanent accommodation is planned. Good news for those of us whose tent

---

* 1 Corinthians 15:35–37.
** Philippians 3:21 (ESV).
*** Matthew 13:43.

pegs are rusting and who need patching up! Every ache and pain will be left behind,

> *For we know that if the earthly tent we live in is destroyed, we have a building from God, an eternal house in heaven, not built by human hands.*

2 CORINTHIANS 5:1–2

CITIZENS OF HEAVEN

A few years ago, an Australian friend, Simon, came to Trevor and I and asked for prayer. Simon had married Ina, from Germany, and they had come to live in the UK. It became clear he was struggling because his identity was split between three countries. As we prayed, we had a picture for him of a passport marked 'Citizen of Heaven'. Here is truth that transcends national boundaries, evicts racism and breaks down the walls between us. As Christians, we can cross great divides because we recognize that we are all foreigners on earth and that our primary identity is this: we are citizens of heaven.

Absorb that and it will change how you live; this is what enabled the great saints to count the cost of loss and persecution,

> *But we are citizens of heaven, where the Lord Jesus Christ lives. And we are eagerly waiting for him to return as our Saviour.*

PHILIPPIANS 3:20 (NLT)

Once you recognize that you are a refugee here, you will want to set eternal goals.

Here is why Abraham could leave all that was familiar to go to the Promised Land; he knew that God had a new home for him. Could the limp ineffectiveness of much of the Western church be because we have lost sight of this? We act as if this life is our home and we have stopped looking ahead to all that God has for us. When we set our eyes on eternity, it is like water on a parched plant for a church that is bereft of anticipation.

Short-sighted faith that avoids talk of heaven will eventually stumble. If we make this earth our home, we inevitably invest in the temporary. I was astonished when I heard that the shop, John Lewis, sold a duvet that cost £10,000. Was it made of diamonds? It points to a culture obsessed with comfort, where our earthly homes matter more than our eternal God. We live differently when we remember that we are citizens of heaven. Our priorities shift when we join Paul and the early church and eagerly await the day of 'the final restoration of all things'* that God promised long ago through his prophets. Here is rescue from the strangling grip of a grab-it-now lifestyle. Here is comfort for the grieving and challenge for the living.

Here is a confession – I am far from a minimalist. We had to downsize when we moved house and our loft was a scary place. With the help of some mighty muscle from church friends, we spent a day hulking the contents downstairs. There was an alarming amount of tat destined for the dump and the charity shop, but we still brought an enormous lorry full with us. At the time, I was reading the book of Hebrews, written at a time of horrendous persecution for Christians. Some of the church had all their possessions removed. Their extraordinary response was to accept the confiscation of their property *'joyfully'* because they knew they had better and lasting possessions.** Can you imagine joyfully losing all your property? This is no Marie-Kondo-style decluttering, this is losing everything. But they knew that what was coming was so much better. When we grasp that, really grasp it, it is utterly liberating.

* Acts 3:21 (NLT).
** Hebrews 10:34.

ETERNAL REWARD

God's economy is different to ours. It is eternal. Jesus says, 'Rejoice and be glad, because great is your reward in heaven!'*

Can you think of the last time you stopped to rejoice about your heavenly reward? If I am honest, before this book, I had rarely thought about laying up treasure in heaven.** Having researched a little, I am still not sure exactly what that treasure looks like, but I am encouraged that all that we have lost will be restored and that every sacrifice for Christ will be rewarded. The Second Coming of Christ will be a refiner's fire and only the gold in our lives will remain, only that which is founded on Jesus.*** The lasting treasure will be those things that we have done on earth which have an eternal impact because they pointed to Christ.

My boys have teased me that two of the earliest words that I taught them were 'delayed gratification'. It is a sign of maturity to be able to wait, motivated by what is ahead, not to eat all the chocolate before breakfast! But we miss out on the greatest motivation of all if we sideline verses like this,

> *Whatever you do, work at it with all your heart, as working for the Lord, not for human masters, since you know that you will receive an inheritance from the Lord as a reward.*

COLOSSIANS 3:23–24

It stirs us to live differently when we see that our words, our gifts, our acts of kindness and our prayers all have eternal repercussions. At the same time, it is tragic that some misguided people have used the idea of eternity as an excuse to abdicate from our calling to be world-changers. They say that if heaven lies ahead, why bother with

---

* Matthew 5:12.
** Matthew 6:19–21.
*** 1 Corinthians 3:13.

the poor, why bother about climate change, why bother to invest in this world? NT Wright demolishes that attitude,

> People who believe in the resurrection, in God making a whole new world in which everything will be set right at last, are unstoppably motivated to work for that new world in the present.[25]

Seeing the destination changes the journey! You will be more secure, take more risks and joy will light up your days if you actively trust the promises that every tear will be tenderly wiped away, that gladness will overtake sorrow in the marathon of life, and that all creation will be renewed. You will be freed to give and forgive. You will be more generous in every way when you know that anything you give up for Jesus will beat the best stocks and shares and be returned with interest. If you take some time to read all the verses that promise you an eternal reward, it will recalibrate you.

I think of my friend Sarah, a Cambridge graduate, who could have chosen a completely different path, but instead spent years working in relative obscurity in DR Congo, helping translate the Bible and sharing her translation skills with the team there at Shalom University in Bunia. Along the way, she faced hair-raising journeys, Ebola nearby, the ongoing threat of militia forces and the death of dear friends. One particularly terrifying incident was when she and her flatmate, MaryAnne, were burgled while in Nairobi,

> 'Three men armed with machetes broke into our house and our bedrooms, leaving us with no time to raise the alarm. They snatched our computers and mobile phones and demanded and took money, lots of it, some of it personal, but most destined for people in Congo, as MaryAnne was about to travel. They were in our rooms for nearly half an hour, and when they had finished, they tied us up. Mercifully, they didn't hurt us, except for giving us the odd slap.'

Sarah was left terribly shaken but yet chose to remain. In a letter she wrote at the time, she quoted from the Psalms,

But I am trusting you, O LORD,
saying, 'You are my God!'
My future is in your hands.

PSALM 31:14–15 (NLT)

Why did Sarah stay? Her eyes were on eternity; she wrote in her letter of 'the hope of the resurrection. Jesus has beaten death, and gives his risen life to his people. Death is just a doorway to never-ending life.'

For most of us, our mission is in our own community or workplace, not overseas, but the knowledge of our eternal destiny can still change our Monday morning, our homes and our work. The headteacher of our local school, where I was chaplain, told me that she would imagine Jesus walking the corridors and then do everything that she could to make the school a place where he knew that he was welcome, whether it was making children and staff feel valued, listening to parents, striving for excellence or setting up a 24-7 prayer room where the children loved to come.

My friend Tristan has an influential role in a city bank. He told me that for him, it changes two things:

'My orientation: When I'm feeling ambitious, I need to ask myself whose kingdom am I building? Am I living for myself or for him? How does that impact how I interact with colleagues and clients? Having an orientation that I am here to build God's kingdom enables me to make choices that might appear countercultural in terms of priorities (e.g., focus on people and not promotion). It drives me to God in prayer through the day. I don't always get things right, but I hope to model humility when I get things wrong and correct myself with the help of God's Spirit.

'My firm foundation: I know that even if I lose my job tomorrow, I am in God's hands. I don't have to fear what others think, or live for man's empty praises which so easily disappoint. When faced with conflict, I can turn to him for peace and direction. My wife is

American and has a close family. When offered an opportunity to work in the US during the summer, I was afraid what others would think, but a Christian colleague challenged me to fear God alone. That has stayed with me as a reminder to do what I believe pleases God and is consistent with doing my job well, even if it is different to others.' (it's all relative I guess) !!!

When our eyes are on eternity, we live differently. The biblical scholar, Gordon Fee, explains how Paul was transformed by the certainty that the resurrection of Jesus guaranteed his own; it gave Paul a unique perspective on suffering which enabled him to 'throw himself into the present with a kind of holy abandon, full of rejoicing and thanksgiving'.[26]

THE BEST IS YET TO COME

Living with the long view transforms our everyday actions and emotions. It has transformed grief for me. While I was away on retreat recently, I saw a picture in my mind's eye of a golden sunrise spilling over the horizon, filling every dark valley with golden light. For me, it was like the promise of eternity which spills over the distant horizon to transform my sorrows. It changes the landscape into colour. My memory of the day that Trevor died is slowly changing from being one of great trauma to a day that is held within the eternal love of God. Whatever traumas you have faced, I pray that will be true for you.

God offers a joy that spills over the distant horizon to reach us in our darkest days. So often that joy comes packaged in promises. I especially treasure this promise that Jesus made, 'If I go and prepare a place for you, I will come back and take you to be with me that you also may be where I am.'* A while ago, one of my sons went to Uganda. The day before he returned, I went into his room and

* John 14:3.

scraped off the layer of dust that had settled while he had been away – I wanted to get it ready for him. What does it mean that God should prepare a place for me and for you? Does God care that personally for us? Not that I imagine God with a heavenly duster; rather my mind is boggled that the architect of the Grand Canyon and the artist of sunset skies could be preparing a home for me. It comforts me that he had prepared a place for Trevor ready for his homecoming. I like to imagine that there was a pair of new running shoes waiting.

Trevor tweeted this just days after his last birthday in August 2017, shortly before he went home to God, 'No eye has seen, no ear has heard, no mind has conceived what God has prepared for those who love him. #Godspromise'*

God has prepared a home for us and it is going to be glorious. In John's gospel, the first miracle that Jesus performs is at a wedding. To the horror of the hosts, the wine runs out. In a culture where a wedding was the biggest celebration of the year, it is a social disaster in the making. Jesus steps in to turn the jars of water into wine that surpasses any vintage that you have ever drunk. The wine taster is astonished that the best has been saved until last. This is what God is like. The best is yet to come.

* From 1 Corinthians 2:9.

RESPONSE:

Why do you think we often ignore the hope of heaven in the Western world?

How does knowing the glory ahead change our present pains? Can you imagine those eternal scales?

Remember a time of great joy or a place of great beauty, then consider what most excites you about heaven. What do you hope for in heaven? Dare to allow yourself to hope.

How would I honestly answer those questions that Tristan asks, 'Whose kingdom am I building? Am I living for myself or for him?'

Can you think of a time when a reward has motivated you? How does it change your priorities when you trust that the best is yet to come?

A PRAYER TO PRAY

Father, today, I praise you that whatever I face, the end of my story is joy. Help me to live in the trust that my troubles are light and momentary compared to the weight of your eternal glory and goodness. Thank you that with you, joy wins. With you, the best is yet to come.

Amen

Chapter 3

Both Sides of the Wall

Now this is eternal life: that they know you,
the only true God, and Jesus Christ, whom you have sent.
JOHN 17:3

There is a fascinating story told by Bede of the conversion of King Edwin of Northumbria from paganism to Christ in the seventh century. The king met with his council, to hear the preaching of the gospel and weigh up the doctrine of this new faith. One council member spoke up and likened life to a sparrow flying swiftly through the great doors at either end of the banqueting hall where the king sat to eat by the fire in the winter. He pointed out that while inside the hall the sparrow was safe from the winter storms,

> but after a few moments of comfort, he vanishes from sight into the wintry world from which he came. Even so, man appears on earth for a little while; but of what went before this life or of what follows, we know nothing.[27]

King Edwin decided to turn to Christ because with his resurrection comes the wonderful reassurance that we too will be raised. Knowing Christ reassures us that death will not win, but, like King Edwin, we still cannot see where the sparrow flies. What exactly will heaven be like? No one has sent us a photo of our eternal home. Scripture helps us to anticipate the joy ahead, but we only see in part what will be. Reading what the Bible says about heaven is a bit like reading a guidebook written in a language that we have only just started to learn.

When our boys were young, we were driving to Cornwall and began talking about heaven. I had a brief moment of delight that no one was squabbling, and the conversation was for once not about football. Then, an argument erupted:

One of the boys said, 'My heaven home is going to have a violin.'

To which his brother replied, 'Well mine is going to have a swimming pool!'

'I'm going to have a swimming pool too!'

'But I thought of that first!'

At which point, it escalated into a shouting match that was anything but heavenly.

We laugh about that now, but it is true that when it comes to envisaging heaven, we are like someone brought up in the Sahara Desert trying to imagine snow, or like someone who has lived their life in the dark trying to imagine colour. There are many unanswered questions. What does Jesus mean when he says we will be like the angels? How could wolves and leopards lie down with lambs and calves and still have the teeth and nature of a carnivore?* Are the gates of the heavenly city literally made out of pearl? What parts of the book of Revelation are metaphorical? And as to the timing of it all, Jesus makes it clear that we are not supposed to know.** Why doesn't the Bible simply tell us in plain terms? I suspect that is because ultimately heaven is so much bigger and more glorious than we can even begin to grasp. How could an embryo imagine life outside of the womb? If my little brain strains when I plan next year's diary, how can I get my head around eternity?

* Matthew 22:30, Isaiah 11:6.
** Matthew 24:23–27; 36, 42, 44.

KNOWING THE WAY

If, like King Edwin and his council, you too struggle to get your head around what is to come, be encouraged that we do not need a 'Heaven Brochure' in our back pockets any more than the Israelites needed a detailed map of the Promised Land. What matters is that we know the way, and when it comes to eternity, that means knowing the One who is the Way. He tells us,

> 'Do not let your hearts be troubled. You believe in God; believe also in me. My Father's house has many rooms; if that were not so, would I have told you that I am going there to prepare a place for you? And if I go and prepare a place for you, I will come back and take you to be with me that you also may be where I am. You know the way to the place where I am going.'

What a relief that Thomas steps in, as usual, representing all of us who are slow on the uptake, 'Lord, we don't know where you are going, so how can we know the way?' Jesus makes it absolutely clear,

> 'I am the way and the truth and the life. No one comes to the Father except through me. If you really know me, you will know my Father as well. From now on, you do know him and have seen him.'

JOHN 14:1–7

'The way' that Jesus talks about is not a series of complex creeds to learn or a set of good deeds to be done; 'the way' is knowing Jesus. The early Christians understood this and called themselves people of 'the Way'. As early as the book of Acts, Saul was trying to persecute the people 'belonging to the Way.'* Knowing the Saviour who is The Way is what makes a Christian.

---

* Acts 9:2.

This is the heart of the gospel; knowing God is the way to eternal life:

'Now this is eternal life: that they know you, the only true God, and Jesus Christ, whom you have sent.'

JOHN 17:3

I used to think that this verse meant that it is through knowing God that I get my 'ticket' to heaven. God is the source of life and so there is no eternal life apart from him, but something deeper is meant here. As Leon Morris writes in his commentary on John's gospel, 'Here we have something of a definition of eternal life. Really to know God is more than the way to life. It is life.'[28]

Eternal life is not only about future hope; it is about our *present* experience of what is to come. Eternal life can begin now because we can know God now. I am too small to fully grasp the enormity of eternity but today I can grasp the hand of my eternal God. I am too dull to comprehend infinity, but I can begin the infinite journey of knowing God right now. Eternal life starts *now*.

THIS SIDE OF THE WALL

In my moments of grief, I needed to know that God meets me this side of eternity. There were times when I found little comfort in the truth that Trevor was with God because I wanted Trevor with me here. It felt as if I was hammering on a wall that I could never get through until I died. As I brought that to God in prayer, I found that God is with me – with me on this side of the wall, with me on this side of eternity.

I wrote this poem in that first year of grief – it is raw because it was the cry of my heart – but I hope that it shares something of the comfort that I found that God is with each one of us on this side of that great divide that is death, understanding the grief, grieving with us in it, and helping us to find new ways to live.

THE WALL

The boundary is a wall too high to climb,
implacable, it stretches on and on
I cannot find the door.
My darling, you are on the other side,
I cannot reach you anymore.

If I batter the stony wall, I bleed and break
frantically, I run and call for you.
The wall stands cold, unyielding
and you are silent too.
Sometimes I'm restless with the longing
to see you walk back in the room
with your smiling eyes that made me feel secure.
I ache to hear your voice, to hold your hand again
I expect you everywhere but you are gone
and I lament.

Decades ago, I biked along a rush-hour road
I never saw the tangling, mangling car
that knocked me off onto the ground
scything, splitting, searing,
tearing tendon and skin apart.
Yet this is harder still
now I am severed from you, my love
so final, so far.

'I lost my husband' sounds so careless.
I care more than I knew,
the compass of my heart keeps seeking you.
But you are gone.

And yet, to my strange surprise
I find not all is lost
across this great divide
for you are with my God
and my God is here with me
on my side of the wall.

Here to hold me, oh so tenderly
I do not grieve alone
for God himself was battered on this wall
split apart, torn to the heart for me.
Now he who cried 'forsaken'
binds up my fractured soul and treasures every tear.

Nothing can withstand such love
the passion of eternity prevails
as Hadrian's might was humbled and East kissed West in old Berlin,
these stones in turn will crumble and God will bring me in
rejoicing in the joy that now fills you.

Still here for a while, still I grieve
grateful for each ray of comfort
a hug, a prayer, a sunrise and a song,
a tin of brownies on the doorstep with my name,
my sons, my friends, new hope
love lighting up new ways for me to be
kaleidoscoping colours from each broken piece of glass
the promise of the dawn after the dark.[29]

If you, too, feel that profound separation of the wall of death, or maybe feel the pain of some other devastating loss, God wants you to know that he is here for you on this side of the wall. Jesus came to be Immanuel, God with you. Here is great comfort: not only do we have a blazingly bright future hope, we have the very present help of knowing God today.

SEE HOW HE LOVES US

God wants us to know his love for us this side of the wall. That means being real with him about our sorrows. Rejoicing in the hope of the glory ahead does not mean that God expects us to glibly deny our present struggles. God does not dismiss our griefs, and neither should we. There is a moment in Chapter 11 of John's gospel that I have grown to treasure, because it destroys any false idea we may have that God expects us to hide our tears and fix on a smile because we know that we are heading to Paradise. Jesus hears that his dear friend, Lazarus, is dead. We might expect Jesus to arrive at the scene and to tell everyone to cheer up because he is going to raise Lazarus back to life. Instead, when he sees the grief of the mourners, Jesus is utterly overcome by grief. In the middle of John's account are two of the most startling words in Scripture: 'Jesus wept'.*

Can this be true – that God wept?

We have a God who weeps with us just as he unashamedly wept with all those who mourned for Lazarus. It is unlikely that it was just a stray tear. I suspect Jesus was sobbing with wrenching tears; his grief made such an impression that the mourners said, 'See how he loved him!' This is the same God who spoke so tenderly through his prophet Isaiah, telling us that he became our Saviour because of his great compassion, 'In all their distress he too was distressed.'**

Here is a profound insight into God's heart, this is the love of God for us; our God comes alongside us, feeling with us as well as acting for us. In my times of deep sorrow, it has enormously helped me to see that even though Jesus knew that the end of the story for Lazarus was resurrection, still he wept. Jesus had already declared to Martha, 'I am the resurrection and the life'!*** and yet he wept. Look ahead a few hours and Jesus will no longer be weeping, he will

* John 11:35.
** Isaiah 63:7–9.
*** John 11:25.

be shouting with a loud voice, 'Lazarus, come out!' and death will be vanquished. The end of the story is joy. Yet still Jesus feels with us and cares for us in our present struggles on this side of the wall. Whatever you face today, he knows that the end of your story is joy, but here and now, God cares so deeply that he weeps with us in our suffering. See how he loves us!

I wonder if you need reminding that God is with you in the present moment, or if you need reminding of the promise of glory ahead? God is on both sides of the wall.

HEAVEN AS A LIFE

It has made all the difference to me to discover that I do not have to wait until I die to know God with me. I treasure the devotional books of nineteenth-century South African minister, evangelist and theologian Andrew Murray, who writes that many Christians think of heaven as the place where they hope to go but miss out on thinking of, 'heaven as a life, and of God's nearness as an experience for every hour of our daily walk.'[30] We can experience the joy of living this life with our God who is utterly good, gloriously beautiful, victoriously strong, unbreakably trustworthy, constant with comfort, mind-bogglingly creative and infinitely loving.

In the ongoing tension that we face between 'now and not yet', the promise of knowing God is a promise for now. It is not all about delayed gratification. Eternal life is knowing and being known by God and that can begin today. I have an unbreakable connection with eternity when I walk through life holding hands with the eternal One. He is invisible but the heart of the Christian message is that he makes himself known to us and there is always more to know!

This side of heaven, God is still working his wonders and performing miracles. At the age of 20, I spent one summer working with St Stephen's Society and Jackie Pullinger in Hong Kong. I shared a room with a little lady, Elfrida, who had been taken into prostitution as a young girl; she did not even know how old she was. God had healed her of her lifelong addiction to heroin, and I watched as he enabled her to smile again. In her seventies, Elfrida was married. Over the years, I have seen again and again that God makes himself known in our lives in ways far beyond our expectations.[31]

My friend Henrik has an amazing story of God's power breaking into his life. In 2016, he was diagnosed with acute myeloid leukaemia. His immune system was barely functioning. The prognosis was dreadful and four gruelling cycles of chemotherapy lay ahead. Henrik decided to trust that he was God's beloved child whatever happened but was given hope when someone sent him this promise, 'I remain confident of this: I will see the goodness of the LORD in the land of the living.'* Henrik says, 'I especially liked the living part!'

In October 2016, Henrik had a stem cell transplant which seemed to work until the spring of 2017, when suddenly his inflammatory markers shot up to 250 (normal is just above 0). As the days passed, his condition worsened. He experienced severe muscle pain and his legs swelled up. He turned yellow, a sign that his liver was under attack. It was so serious that Henrik's wife, Inger, called a prayer meeting of all their friends. On 12 July 2017, 20 people gathered in their front room and about another 60 people around the world on their WhatsApp group prayed for him. At the end of the evening, Henrik felt peace, although the pain was still there. He writes,

'Everyone went home and that was that. But when I woke up the next morning, I realized all the pain was gone, and whereas before I had trouble even getting downstairs, I actually had half a day at Wimbledon women's semi-finals with my daughter Harriet! I suspected God had healed me but it was not until I took the next tests and the inflammatory markers were normal that the penny fully dropped. Since that day I have not had any symptoms, not a ripple on any graph. Every doctor tells me how amazing these results are! They say it's as if I had never been sick.'

* Psalm 27:13.

God made himself known to Henrik and Inger, through healing. For Elfrida, it was in her release from pain and addiction. For us, it was in our grief. Wherever we are, God wants to make himself known to us. He wants us to know his goodness in the land of the living.

MISSING THE TREASURE

What a tragedy if we were to miss the offer of knowing the One who has loved us before the world began and who will love us for all eternity. We live in the days that the prophets longed for!

> 'For truly I tell you, many prophets and righteous people longed to see what you see but did not see it, and to hear what you hear but did not hear it.'

MATTHEW 13:17

Some years ago, I noticed a painting hanging on the wall of my parents' home and decided to research the signature. I was thrilled to discover that the artist had some paintings displayed in the prestigious Musée d'Orsay in Paris. My parents had it valued and it ended up paying for a wonderful family holiday after it had been restored. It had needed significant work because it had been hanging over the fireplace which hosts a roaring fire each winter. My mum and dad had no clue as to its value. I wonder how often we overlook the treasure that is God himself?

We have the priceless treasure box of the gospels, written that we might know our Saviour, not just as a historical idea or dry doctrine but in a personal relationship with the risen Lord. The gospels are full of stories of flawed, real people meeting God – written so that we can meet him ourselves. They are accounts of encounters because God is inviting us to have our own encounter with him. So, when Jesus asks Peter, 'Who do you say I am?',* every

* Matthew 16:15.

reader is asked that question too. When Jesus challenges Martha, 'everyone who lives and believes in me shall never die. Do you believe this?', Jesus is asking us whether we believe it too. Can we reply with Martha, 'Yes, Lord; I believe that you are the Christ, the Son of God, who is coming into the world.'?*

As we read God's Word, Jesus beckons us into a relationship that will change the trajectory of our lives. In the coming chapters, we will see how this relationship with our eternal God can grow. It's not like learning all the words in a dictionary. As Leon Morris writes, 'The point is surely valid that Jesus has in mind an ever-increasing knowledge, not something given in its completeness once and for all.'[32]

OUR SELF-REVEALING GOD

No one can see God in all his blazing glory** but the overarching story of Scripture is that God so wants to make himself known to us that he reveals himself to us.

We can never find God on our own. I remember gazing at the stars in Snowdonia and struggling to absorb the reality that my eyes were scanning light years. When my son Connor was younger, he asked, 'What's the universe expanding into?' If I struggle to answer that, how can my tiny brain possibly know the One who holds infinity in the palm of his hand? We can never know God without his help. Only through God can we know God.

Here is the heart of the gospel,

> No one has ever seen God, but the one and only Son, who is himself God and is in closest relationship with the Father, has made him known.

JOHN 1:18

* John 11:26–27 (ESV).
** 1 Timothy 6:16.

The biblical scholar Craig Keener puts it beautifully, when he writes that Jesus is the 'perfect revealer', who 'unveils God's character absolutely.'[33]

God makes God known to us and wonderfully this knowledge does not involve taking exams! Eternal life is not merely knowing *about* God, even the demons can do that.* I have taken more than enough exams, so I say hurray that we do not have to be high-flying intellectuals to know God! The offer of eternal life entails knowing God like I know those I live with, like I know my boys, like I knew Trevor. It speaks of the deepest intimacy. My friend Sheena beautifully describes intimacy as 'into-me-see'; that is what God wants with us. No more hiding like Adam and Eve did in the garden, no more shame! God offers himself to us, waiting for us to open our hearts to him.

FRIENDS WITH GOD

God offers to be my friend, to be your friend through the joys and the sorrows. It is worth asking what would make us struggle with that? Do we feel unworthy? Jesus promised to make himself known to the disciples even though he knew that they would fail him. Like every great promise of Scripture, the promise of God's friendship depends on his mercy and not our deserving.

If we miss out on God's friendship, it is always because we withdraw. Perhaps we have not grasped his mercy. Perhaps we are chasing other distractions. Perhaps we expect too little from God. Perhaps it is because social media sets a low bar for intimacy. You can have thousands of 'friends' and never speak to them from year to year. God deserves more than to be thrown the occasional virtual 'like'. He wants to share our homes, our lives and the desires of our hearts.

* James 2:19.

Satan whispers that God is distant, like a divine watchmaker who set the world ticking only to step back into the distant ether and let it run on its own. Jesus hurls that lie into oblivion with these words,

> *I no longer call you servants, because a servant does not know his master's business. Instead, I have called you friends, for everything that I learned from my Father I have made known to you.*

JOHN 15:15

What must John have felt when he heard that? At the Last Supper, John was so close to Jesus that he was leaning up against him,[*] like my sons would do when we watched TV. Since the world pandemic, people have had to learn what social distancing is, but God is not socially distant. Today, God invites us to be the kind of friend that John was, so close that we can lean up against him, so close that he shares his heart with us.

I am bemused and overwhelmingly blessed by the truth that God wants to know me as a friend. Since losing Trevor, I treasure it all the more. God is here with me when I take a cup of coffee into the garden, to help me plan my holidays and to listen to me about my work stress, to share my hopes and to comfort me when I am sad. God is here to be our closest friend. We are invited to lean on our beloved friend – that is how we make our way out of the desert times, 'Who is this coming up from the wilderness leaning on her beloved?'[**]

GOD GIVES US A HEART TO KNOW HIM

God, the eternal God, wants to make himself known to us this side of the wall, not through some long-distance correspondence course but close enough to lean on, near enough to know. He gives us his

[*] John 13:23.
[**] Song of Songs 8:5.

Spirit of revelation to make that happen. That is why Paul prays unceasingly,

> *I keep asking that the God of our Lord Jesus Christ, the glorious Father, may give you the Spirit of wisdom and revelation so that you may know him better.*

EPHESIANS 1:17

We too can ask God for his Spirit of revelation. We never have to twist God's arm or jump hurdles to know him; this is what God longs for.

Look at the very start, before the world was spoiled; God chooses to walk and talk with Adam and Eve in the garden – to make himself known to them. Trace through the books of the Bible and you will see a God who wants to show us who he is. From the moment that he told Abraham his name to the moment that he became flesh in Jesus, God has been making himself known. Trace through the Old Testament and you will see God sharing his names which show us his character. God spoke to Moses, face to face, as a friend, and God wants to do the same with us.* In every inspired word of Scripture, we see God's longing that we would know him. This longing to be known is at the heart of God's promise of a new covenant agreement with us; God speaks through the prophet Jeremiah saying, 'I will give them a heart to know me, that I am the LORD. They will be my people, and I will be their God.'**

I am sometimes sluggish in my pursuit of knowing God, so I love that verse from Jeremiah. God offers us new hearts that *want* to know him. It is the core component of the new agreement that he makes with his people,

---

* Exodus 33:11.
** Jeremiah 24:7.

'I will put my law in their minds
    and write it on their hearts.
I will be their God,
    and they will be my people.
No longer will they teach their neighbour,
    or say to one another, "Know the LORD,"
because they will all know me,
from the least of them to the greatest,'

JEREMIAH 31:33–34

This promise is not only for the elite; it is a promise for *all* and that includes you and me.

This is the heart of the gospel. The offer to know God is not only an Old Testament promise; it is central to why Christ was born, died, rose and ascended.[*] Jesus prays for his disciples, saying to his Father,

'I have made you known to them and will continue to make you known in order that the love you have for me may be in them and that I myself may be in them.'

JOHN 17:26

This is the culmination, the goal, the great aim; we were made for this – to know and to be known by God.

As ever with God, all is gift; Jesus promises that the Holy Spirit will share the greatest treasure of all – himself, 'for he will take what is mine and declare it to you.'[**] Some people are like a locked door; they refuse to give themselves to you. God is the opposite. In my room, I have a treasured gift, a picture with some beautiful calligraphy by Cath Sales with these words: *'The Holy Spirit will take what is mine and make it known to you.'* It hangs in my room,

---

* Hebrews 8:8-12.
** John 16:14 (ESV).

a reminder that it is by God that we know God – that the door is open. In the chapters ahead, we will discover that here is a home with many rooms where we are invited to linger, to dwell and to explore.

Like every sure promise of God, it is there to be made into a prayer. 'Father, give me your Holy Spirit, to make what is yours known to me.' Could you make that your prayer as you read on through this book? Ask the everlasting God to make himself known to you this side of the wall. He will.

> *'The Holy Spirit will take what is mine and make it known to you.'*

RESPONSE

Begin by quietening your heart. As Andrew Murray writes,

> We do not give God enough time to reveal himself… we forget that one of the very first things in prayer is to be silent.[34]

If your mind is racing, pause, breathe and deliberately lift the eyes of your heart to God.

Jesus asks you, 'Who do you say I am?'* How will you reply?

God is your friend. What would you like to talk to him about? It might be something big, but you might just want to have a chat and tell him about one small thing you have enjoyed this week – a walk, a meal or a friend you saw? Remember, he likes your company.

---

* Matthew 16:15.

Spend some time thinking about God's promise that you will know his goodness in the land of the living. If you are in a particularly hard time at the moment, trust him that you are still his beloved child.

Do you sometimes overlook the treasure that is on offer – the treasure of knowing God? What might God want you to see that you have overlooked?

A PRAYER

Thank you, loving Father, for the sure promise that we will know you. Today, I ask you for your Spirit of revelation that I might know you better. Please give me your Holy Spirit, to make what is yours known to me.

Amen

Chapter 4

Gazing on God

I have set the LORD *always before me;*
PSALM 16:8 (ESV)

This great call to know the eternal God, begins and continues with gazing on God. He gazes back with such love in his eyes that we long for the day when we will be face to face. As John Henry Newman wrote long ago, all the greatest wonders of the world are like an atom put next to the grandeur of gazing on God; 'it is the occupation of eternity.'[35]

Yet so often we look the other way. Life offers multiple distractions! Little frustrations buzz and bite like mosquitoes. Worries jostle for prime position and brain-space gets crowded. If it is not the state of the world, a tricky relationship can totally sabotage our peace. There are bills to pay and there is social media to preoccupy us. Even our God-given dreams can push God out of the picture and tightly held goals can become more important than God. Whether I wake bright-eyed or bleary, there is a to-do list to greet me, which in my case, too regularly includes things that I should have done yesterday. In the midst of it all, the Almighty God is calling for our attention.

SETTING THE LORD BEFORE US

My dad used to take a daily walk in the woods with their golden retriever to the same shady copse where he would stop to pray. One day, he was busily running through a list of concerns and God interrupted. God said to him, 'I want your attention!' Although he doesn't remember this now, or what it was that God wanted to say to him, I have never forgotten him relating this story, and it changed my attitude to prayer. What an extraordinary thing that the God of the universe should stoop down and say to us, 'I want your attention!'

It turns out that we have a part to play in the process of becoming eternally minded. God wants us involved in this outrageously unequal partnership in which he is the source and the end of the revelation. Our part is so simple – to give him our attention, to say with King David,

'I have set the LORD always before me.'

PSALM 16:8 (ESV)

How do we set the Lord before us?

The writer and speaker, Mary Kissell,[36] has a simple but memorable phrase that has helped me with this: 'It only takes a moment to turn.' It only takes a moment to turn your attention to the Lord, to acknowledge that God is near. Like a vacuum, our heads fill up with other stuff if we do not intentionally turn our attention to the Lord. We have to consciously and conscientiously turn our love and affection towards him, to gaze on the One who loves us with an unwavering love.

We set the Lord before us by recognizing that he is here with us, right now. As the great eighteenth-century preacher, John Wesley, said in his final hours, 'The best of all is, God is with us!'[37]

The risen Jesus is here, now, in the room and in the words of that great teacher on prayer, Brother Lawrence, we are called to practise the presence of God, to deliberately remind ourselves that God is near.

At which point, you might say, that is fine for Brother Lawrence who seemed to spend a lot of time washing up and peeling vegetables; it is not too hard to recall God's presence when I am doing mundane tasks. But what if my job demands full concentration? What about the orthopaedic surgeon? It could be disastrous if her attention was not fully on wielding her scalpel.

We cannot constantly keep our conscious thought on God but we can nurture an underlying trust that the One who loves us best is with us. Brother Lawrence found that as he cultivated the practice of God's presence, his mind would naturally return to God after a time of busyness. As I write this, I am in the same room as my family. My attention is on my writing while deep down I am comforted by knowing they are here with me. The point is that our relationships would fracture if I never gave them concentrated attention. Our family's closeness is built around the times when we focus on each other, listen and give each other eye contact. If we never did that, we would become distant.

In just the same way, we need times when we deliberately set the Lord before us. Today, lots of things will be shouting at you, 'I want your attention!' Will you listen for that quiet voice of the One who loves you best of all, asking you to turn the eyes of your heart to him? Will you take a moment to turn? Because when you give him your attention, you will find that you already have his.

God is waiting for us in his Word, inviting us to join the Psalmist and pray, daily, 'Open my eyes, that I may see wonderful things in your law.'* In the early days after Trevor died, I had many broken nights; desperation more than devotion sent me to God, but I found comfort as I reached for my Bible. There were no instant answers but as I look back over my prayer journal, I have a record of how

---

* Psalm 119:18.

God spoke to me in those dark hours. God wants our attention. Jesus says,

> 'Here's what I want you to do: Find a quiet, secluded place so you won't be tempted to role-play before God. Just be there as simply and honestly as you can manage. The focus will shift from you to God, and you will begin to sense his grace.'

MATTHEW 6:6 (MSG)

WHEN THE FOG DESCENDS

But what about when God seems absent? I know I am not alone in that experience. Why would God allow that? Increasingly, I realize that there is no simple answer to this question. It varies from person to person and from season to season in our lives. For me, when God seems distant, it takes time to work out whether the issue is with me or whether something else is going on.

I have found that a good starting point is to ask God to search my heart. Sometimes, there is stuff in the way – idols to topple, sins to confess, people to forgive, forgiveness to receive. I have too often given airtime to Satan's lies that God does not care or that he would not forgive me instead of receiving the grace that always welcomes me when I come home to my Father.

But even after turning to God as well as I am able, there have been moments when prayer has been like ringing a doorbell that no-one bothers to answer. Why would God make us wait to find him? Looking back on some of my apparently barren prayer times, I can see that God was dismantling my false ideas about who he is, refusing to let me go into automatic mode when it comes to prayer. Could it be that God sometimes makes us wait for him because he does not want us to go through the motions mechanically, pushing us to the place where we seek him for himself and not as a solution?

In the past few years, I have discovered another huge reason that God can seem distant. It is hard to sense God when sadness and trauma are filling your headspace. In the months after Trevor's death, I found that quietening my heart before God was scary because stopping meant facing the grief. Raw emotions tend to be confusing and it was difficult to compartmentalize grief away from stress and fear. When I was moving house and changing jobs, the stress of it all shouted even more loudly that Trevor was absent. It can be hard to see God clearly when you are in a fog of emotion.

My son, Connor, did his music degree near the green hills of the South Downs and reckons that it is the most beautiful place in the world. During his last week of university, we went for a final trek together to the highest viewpoint. The National Trust website describes it as a legendary beauty spot, showcasing it with a panoramic photo of the rolling hills at sunset. As we drove up, the cloud thickened into such heavy fog that I almost missed the sign for the car park. We got out of the car and all I could see behind Connor was a sludge-grey swirl of cloud. At that point, I could have decided that the view did not exist, but I trusted the photos from the National Trust website, and I trust Connor. God spoke to me in the midst of that fog, reminding me that he is always there, even when I cannot see him. Even when the fog blots out our view of God, we can trust that he is still there, and his love never fails.

LOOKING IN THE RIGHT DIRECTION

The Bible constantly challenges us to choose where we turn our attention:

> … *whatever is right, whatever is pure, whatever is lovely, whatever is admirable – if anything is excellent or praiseworthy, think about such things.*

PHILIPPIANS 4:8

David said, 'I will set before my eyes no vile thing.'* Instead, he set the Lord always before him. What do we set before us? Usually, it is shaped like a rectangle. The average Brit spends a decade of their lives watching TV, so it is worth evaluating what fills our minds and the minds of our children. By the age of 18, most children have watched around 200,000 violent acts on TV even though the link between screen violence and behaviour is blindingly clear. The impact of pornography is equally concerning, corroding intimacy in relationships.[38]

Does that mean we should bin our screens? What does it mean in practice to think about whatever is pure and praiseworthy? Hiding from the world? Disengaging? Could it be that instead God is calling us to spend time dreaming of what the world looks like when he is enthroned as King, a world where justice prevails? As we will see in the chapters ahead, disengagement is not an option. Keeping our eyes on what is pure and lovely never means hiding from poverty and injustice, whether it is local or on the grand scale of unjust world debt and systemic racism. Instead, we can be inspired by those who have been captivated by a vision of God's kingdom coming to earth, who adopted orphans, started schools and hospitals, stood up for slaves and advocated for the persecuted. When we keep our eyes on the God who loved the world enough to die for it, we will engage with it. God is calling us to fuel our vision with holy imagination and act accordingly.

Christians throughout history have done this. Just one example is the Barnetts who helped transform a slum in Victorian London. Henrietta Barnett was an heiress who married a clergyman called Samuel Barnett. Rather than choosing the high life, they served in Whitechapel where they helped thousands of families, setting up work schemes for women driven by poverty into prostitution and sending children on holidays. They helped build tree-lined roads and access to green spaces. God calls us to follow their example

* Psalm 101:3 (NIV, UK 1984).

and to see a vision for what could be in our streets, in our nation and in our world! Gazing on God never means withdrawing from the real world. As we know him better, we want to be like him. He is never afraid to roll up his sleeves and get dirty in order to clean up the mess. Gazing on God always propels us into the world to be ambassadors of his eternal kingdom.

But first we have to take time to gaze.

LOOKING WITH YOUR ARMS OPEN

> I look: morning to night I am never done with looking
> Looking I mean not just standing around,
> but standing around as though with your arms open.

MARY OLIVER[39]

When did you last look with your arms wide open? How many of us live life with our eyes down, staring at a phone, missing out on the presence of God? Exodus Chapter 3 tells the story of a burning bush. Moses stops and walks towards it and we are told, 'When the LORD saw that he had gone over to look, God called him from within the bush, "Moses, Moses!"' It is only when Moses draws close to look that God reveals himself as 'I am who I am', the One who is ever-present, who is all that we desire and require. It makes me wonder if others had walked past the burning bush and missed it. Maybe God is always waiting for those who will come across and look.

The Lord is near. Let's not miss him.

Let's not miss the Ever-Present One in the cries of the suffering. I do not want Jesus to say to me on the final day, 'I was hungry, and you didn't feed me. I was a Syrian refugee and you didn't clothe me. You missed me.'

The Lord is near. Let's not miss God's glory blazing in his creation. God's fingerprint is there on the distant purple mountain rising above bright waters. His whisper is in the wild winds that make the waves crash. Ezekiel tells us that he is 'Like the appearance of a rainbow in the clouds on a rainy day'* – when we see the golden light around a rainbow, we get a glimpse of God. When I find myself welcomed by the muted yellow of a lowly primrose or warmed by the rich velvet red of a rose, when my heart soars at a mountain peak or is stilled by a stream, when my eyes play over a paint-splashed butterfly wing or scan the stars – all is a gift of his beauty, a ray from his Son, a sentence from the Word, a fragrance of him. It all makes sense when I find that the Maker is behind it all.

> The world is charged with the grandeur of God.
> It will flame out, like shining from shook foil

GERARD MANLEY HOPKINS[40]

Such beauty is incomprehensible without God. Without him, why do we find beauty in places that are not vaguely conducive to survival – in the barren desert of Namibia, in the black volcanic rocks of Giant's Causeway, in a lightning storm, a gnarled tree, a wrinkled smile? As Annie Dillard writes, 'unless all ages and races of men have been deluded by the same mass hypnotist (who?), there seems to be such a thing as beauty, a grace wholly gratuitous.'[41] When we gaze, we see, 'The whole world sparks and flames.'[42] There is such fire that it makes us seek water, such beauty that it points us to the Great Artist. Let's not miss him.

Let's not miss his promises that light up our lives with hope, illuminating us with his holy Word. Or walk past forgiveness offered by nail-pierced hands. Or rush by his tenderness, found in little kindnesses that lift our days. His love is in the sweet surprise of laughter and in the friend who shares our struggles. God is Giver of all and the greatest gift. Let's not miss him.

* Ezekiel 1:28.

Moses came across to look. That first look led him to many days gazing on God's shining face until his face reflected God's glory. Today, we are invited to come with eyes and hearts wide open to do the same.

The bush is blazing. God is ever-present. Let's not miss him.

GAZE ON THE BEAUTY OF THE LORD

One thing I ask from the LORD,
this only do I seek:
that I may dwell in the house of the LORD
all the days of my life,
to gaze on the beauty of the LORD
and to seek him in his temple.

PSALM 27:4

Nothing compares to the beauty of the Lord. It is beyond the greatest beauty in our astounding world. Do you remember that when Moses asked to see the glory of God, God showed him his goodness? What is the ultimate display of God's glorious goodness? It is '…displayed in the face of Christ'.* We too can pray, 'Father, show me your goodness', knowing that God will show us his glory in the face of Jesus.

GOD'S GLORY IS DISPLAYED IN THE FACE OF CHRIST

The Son is the radiance of God's glory

HEBREWS 1:3

---

* 2 Corinthians 4:6.

If you want to see the glory of the beauty of the Lord, gaze at Jesus. There at his incarnation – God cast in spirals of human DNA, we see the beauty of God the infinite, there in a fragment, humbly laying all down for love.

In every gospel snapshot of Christ, we see the beauty of the Lord. This is the God of Isaiah 61 who proclaims good news to the poor and proclaims the year of God's favour. He tenderly binds up the broken-hearted. He proclaims freedom for the captives – what could be more beautiful than our loving God setting people free from sin and sickness, fear and rejection, hopelessness and addiction?

Before our Lord, the idol of physical beauty comes tumbling down. The beauty industry is worth 500 billion dollars worldwide, to our self-obsessed society, shockingly more than our aid budgets. Untold hours are wasted manufacturing the perfect image on social media. There has been a rise in rhinoplasty, which is nothing to do with rhinos; it is cosmetic surgery for noses. Why? Because like a trick mirror, selfies on phones distort the shape of your nose so people are having painful surgery to have their noses reshaped. It would be comic if it was not so tragic. Jesus liberates us from the destructive pursuit of physical perfection. When God came to visit, the prophet Isaiah tells us that he had no beauty by earthly standards.[*] Seen through the distorting spectacles of Western values, his beauty is easy to miss. But look closely and at the ugliest moment of all, there is the glory of God on a bloodied cross. At the depths of human depravity, we see the beauty of the Lord in the ultimate display of his love.

Gaze on Christ, crucified, risen and ascended, shining with glory, lovingly interceding for us – there is the beauty of the Lord.

[*] Isaiah 53:2.

TRANSFORMED AS WE GAZE

When we gaze at God, we discover that his face shines on us with great love, smiling with sheer delight. When we gaze on him, we shine too, 'Those who look to him are radiant; their faces are never covered in shame.' As we gaze, we see that God is for us, not against us. David's desire was to gaze on God, and so he could say, 'though war break out against me, even then I will be confident.'* There is no greater remedy for lack of confidence than seeking God's face.

One of my boys struggled with anxiety as a teenager; he used to get especially nervous with train platforms. At a Christian conference, he was in a youth meeting of about 500 people and a complete stranger gave out a specific word with his name and his age and the promise that God would give him courage. Over the next few years, he began worshipping God, gazing on God every night before going to sleep, and it transformed him.

As we gaze on the Lord, our fears shrink. The Psalmist calls us to magnify the Lord.** Too often, what I place under my internal magnifying glass is the stuff that makes me anxious. Nothing reassures me like gazing on God. When we gaze on him, everything is given an eternal perspective.

THE ONE THING NEEDFUL

Jesus himself said that giving him attention is the one thing we need above all others. Luke tells the story in Chapter 10 of his gospel. Jesus has come to supper with his friends, Martha and Mary, and Martha is terribly distracted with trying to produce a meal for everyone. Her sister, Mary, is sitting at the feet of Jesus so Martha goes to Jesus and grumpily tells him to get her sister to help.

* For a bible study on gazing on God, look at Numbers 6:24–27, Psalm 34:5, Psalm 27:3–4.
** Psalm 34:3 (ESV).

I completely understand where Martha is coming from. I identify with being distracted and I know what it is like to have a mini strop about doing too much housework compared to everyone else. As one who can get hot and bothered making scrambled eggs, Martha has my sympathy. She is slaving in the kitchen and what is deeply aggravating is that her sister is sitting around doing nothing. But the Lord does not give her the response she is seeking, 'Martha, Martha, you are anxious and troubled about many things, but one thing is necessary. Mary has chosen the good portion, which will not be taken away from her.'*

Few passages wind people up as much as this one. People have come up to me and said, 'It's all very well, but there are jobs to do! If Martha hadn't been there, they would have all been hungry!' Sermons sometimes divide people into Marys and Marthas, asking the question, 'Are you contemplative or are you practical?' But that is to take the passage out of context. If we read the whole Bible, it is clear that we are all called to both prayer and action. James says that faith without works is dead. Jesus will say to those who did not care for the poor, 'I never knew you!'** He regularly withdrew to pray but he was highly practical – he washed dirty feet, he fed the hungry and his first miracle was solving a catering problem at a wedding. We may by nature be weighted to either prayer or action but we are all called to both.

The account in Luke is not about personality types, it is about priorities. Martha is offered the attention of the God who made the universe and she puts other things first. It is easy for us to miss how radical it was that Jesus was willing to teach Martha and Mary although they were women! Even today, there are around 65 million girls in the world who are not allowed to go through school; yet 2,000 years ago, Jesus invited Martha and Mary to sit at his feet – the place where a disciple sat before a rabbi. Did that affront

* Luke 10:41–42 (ESV).
** James 2:17, Matthew 7:23.

Martha? Did she think Mary should keep to a woman's place in the kitchen? Either way, Jesus is not happy that Martha refused his invitation. When the Lord of the universe is in the house offering to teach you, you can leave the washing up till later.

Instead, Martha thought that she could tell Jesus what to do. In essence, she says, 'Make my sister help!' Generally, it is a bad plan to try to order God about. Yet Martha did not get it completely wrong. She could have nursed her frustration and run away; instead she went to the Lord. Ever patient, he does not dismiss her; he never does. When we come to Christ with our ragged prayers, he accepts us as we are and then helps to untangle us.

Jesus responds to Martha with words that reveal his care for her heart, 'Martha, you are anxious and troubled about many things'. He knows us better than anyone else, better than we know ourselves. He understood that Martha's frustration was part of a far deeper angst. As my mother has wisely and sometimes annoyingly said to me, 'The issue is not the issue.' Sometimes, it takes time at the feet of Jesus to discover what the real issue is. God wants to care for our hearts.

Some time ago, I spoke on this story and invited people to see themselves at the feet of Jesus. Afterwards, someone told me how she met with God that day. Her mother had died when she was a child and she had buried the pain for years. At the last minute, I had suddenly felt that I should change the song for the ministry time to 'What a Friend we have in Jesus'. I didn't know that it was one of her mother's favourite hymns and that it would bring back memories of a little girl who used to creep downstairs after her bedtime to listen to her mother singing it. She had grown up to be like Martha, busy and active, but during that prayer time, she found herself sitting at Jesus' feet like Mary, her face against his knee. She felt Jesus stroking her hair with the tenderness of a mother, and heard God telling her that he loved her. The next day, she woke up full of bubbling joy, singing, 'I am a child of God.'

Gazing on God is the one thing needful, the thing to place at the top of our daily to-do lists. Perhaps, you might want to literally do that and put time with God in your diary. If you look at the week ahead, where is the time set aside to gaze on God? If, as Augustine insightfully said, sin is being curved in on yourself, then the opposite is to lift our eyes and gaze on God. This is what we were made for.

How we do the one thing needed looks different for all of us; what matters is turning our attention and directing our love daily to God. Nothing helps us to keep that great commandment, to love him, more than setting him before us. Mother Teresa said that you only keep your lamp burning if you fuel it. Gazing is how we fuel our love for God. As CS Lewis wrote, we are to be,

> ... fully God-centred, asking of God no gift more urgently than his presence, than the gift of himself, joyous to the highest degree and unmistakably real.[43]

A gaze is more than a glance. To gaze is to take time to look and appreciate, to explore with your eyes, to know someone better. This is why Moses asked to see God's glory, why David said that it was the one thing he asked for above all others. Nothing compares to the surpassing worth of knowing God.[*]

WELCOMED INTO THE HOLY PLACE

Not long after Trevor died, my dear friend Sonja joined him in glory. She had mentioned aches and pains but none of us expected her to die of a brain tumour just weeks later. Before her death, I nervously went to visit her in the hospice only to find that the Lord's presence was tangible and heaven was near. As I read Psalm 27 to Sonja, she joined in from memory,

---

[*] Philippians 3:8.

One thing I ask from the LORD,
     this only do I seek:
that I may dwell in the house of the LORD
     all the days of my life,
to gaze on the beauty of the LORD
     and to seek him in his temple.

PSALM 27:4

The lightest of gauze voile curtains hung over the French doors in her room; through them, you could see bright sunshine on the water flowing into a pool in the courtyard. Her friend Amanda wrote to me afterwards of 'the living water and the brilliant light the veil reveals behind.'

Too often, I have lived as if there were a concrete partition, not a torn veil between me and the eternal. As if Jesus had not died. As if the Holy of Holies in the temple were still barred by an impenetrable curtain. As if I had not been invited in. But, 'we have confidence to enter the Most Holy Place by the blood of Jesus, by a new and living way, opened for us through the curtain, that is his body'* and so we can know today that we are welcomed into the throne room of God to know his face shining on us. As Andrew Murray writes, 'Jesus secures not only our entrance, but our abiding there.'[44]

What greater blessing is there than the infinite joy of gazing on God? Jonathan Edwards beautifully describes the love of God as an 'exhaustless fountain' for,

We can never by soaring and ascending come to the height of it
We can never by descending come to the depth of it
or by measuring, know the length and breadth of it.

JONATHAN EDWARDS[45]

* Hebrews 10:19–20.

A PRAYER

Lord, how can I ever praise you enough that I can enter the Holy Place and gaze on your glory? I don't want to live my life with eyes fixed on other things when you are ever-present. I am sorry that I so quickly curve in on myself. Please be the lifter of my head. Thank you that when I gaze on you, your face shines on me with love and mercy.

Amen

Be thou my vision, O Lord of my heart;
Naught be all else to me, save that thou art
Thou my best thought, by day or by night;
Waking or sleeping, thy presence my light.

TO CONSIDER

What claims your attention? What fuels your internal clamour and drowns out God's voice?

It is easier to gaze on God when the burning bush blazes bright but what about when life is mundane, when the bush looks dull and there are jobs that need doing? What helps you keep attentive to the Lord on Monday morning? A reminder on your phone?

What fuels your love for God?

What comes to mind when you think of the beauty of God?

Is there a vision that God wants to give you for your home, your street, your city or your nation?

Thank God that he cares for your heart, that he knows your worries and your anxieties. You might want to write a list of them and hand them to him. Magnify him above them all.

Read the story of Martha and Mary in Luke chapter 10. See yourself sitting at Jesus' feet like Mary and ask him what he wants to say to you.

PART 2

Knowing the God of Forever

Each of the chapters ahead are a meditation on the eternal nature of God. They are designed to be read reflectively, expecting to meet with the Living God, allowing his Word to reshape our flawed perceptions of who he is. There is infinitely more of God to be known than this book can hold, but I pray that these reflections will help you to seek and know God better. Knowing him is eternal life.

Before you begin each chapter, here is a prayer to pray:

Glorious Father,
Thank you for your promise to make yourself known to me.
Please pour out your Spirit of wisdom and revelation that I
may know you better
for I come to you, clothed in grace, in the name of your Son,
Jesus Christ,
Amen

Chapter 5

Eternally Mindful

'You are the God who sees me,'
GENESIS 16:13

Never was there a sinner that was half so eager for Christ as Christ is eager for the sinner; nor a saint one-tenth so anxious to behold his Lord as his Lord is to behold him.
CHARLES HADDON SPURGEON[46]

As we begin our journey of gazing on God, what better place to begin than with the wonderful truth that our God eternally gazes on us? In my stumbling journey to be eternally minded, a life-changer has been the discovery that God is eternally mindful of me. In my struggle to remember to turn, to give him my attention, it is both astonishing and wonderful to realize that he never forgets to give his attention to me. It is utterly extraordinary that the almighty God should set his eternal gaze on us.

> *When I consider your heavens,*
> *   the work of your fingers,*
> *the moon and the stars,*
> *   which you have set in place,*
> *what is mankind that you are mindful of them,*
> *   human beings that you care for them?*

PSALM 8:3–4

Can you imagine the shepherd boy David lying under the star-strewn sky on a clear night, his heart bursting with worship as he sang that song? What does it mean that God is mindful of us? Many schools now offer mindfulness sessions, encouraging pupils to still themselves and repeatedly return their attention to the present moment. God repeatedly returns his attention to us. A while ago, I received an email from eBay with the following subject line, 'You are always on our mind Kate.' Somehow, I think not. I am yet to notice eBay's corporate mind showing any personal interest in the highs and lows of my life. Not so with God. You and I are always on God's mind. Because God loves you, he is always thinking about you, waiting for you to think of him. Nothing distracts him. You are the apple of his eye.[*]

> You may fear that the Lord has passed you by, but it is not so: he who counts the stars and calls them by their names is in no danger of forgetting his own children; he knows your case as thoroughly as if you were the only creature he ever made, or the only saint he ever loved. Approach him and be at peace.

CHARLES HADDON SPURGEON[47]

Just in the same way as David marvelled in Psalm 8, we can find all that hard to take in. Can it be true that the God of the heavens is eternally mindful of us? Surely God has more important things to deal with than my petty problems? What about climate change and global poverty? Can I bother God with my sore back or my tricky boss? Such typically British self-deprecation sounds harmless but cloaks subtle lies – it says that God is too busy or too weak to help us. It is as if we envisage God as an air traffic controller with so many planes to keep in the air that he might get distracted and let one crash if I asked him to untangle my kite. As if God has limited time or limited capacity! The Creator of the galaxies is never overloaded.

[*] Psalm 17:8.

Jesus asked, 'Are not two sparrows sold for a penny? Yet not one of them will fall to the ground outside your Father's care. And even the very hairs of your head are all numbered. So don't be afraid; you are worth more than many sparrows.'*

Sparrows cost pennies in the time of Jesus; they were barely worth a second glance. If God notices them, we can be sure that he notices every little detail of our lives. God loves us so dearly that he numbers the hairs on our heads. You need to look close up to do that. God is not sitting on a distant cloud, straining to spot you through a pair of binoculars, trying to find you in a photograph of an entire school. God is near and wants to be involved in our lives.

AN EVER-PRESENT HELP

When I was a child, my parents often had a crowd for Sunday lunch. One week, my mum realized that she had no bread for the meal and no cream to go with the pudding. The shops were shut so she prayed that God would provide some bread. She thought that it would be pushing it to ask for cream too. The doorbell rang; a friend had made fresh bread; the loaf was still warm. Moments later, the guest arrived for lunch, bearing a tub of clotted cream from her holiday in Cornwall. I still find myself astonished that God should care enough to attend to such little details of our lives. If God cares enough to help with a Sunday lunch, how much more does he care about the huge things that we face?

It is because God sees us that he is our ever-present help in times of trouble – in tangible, practical ways.** I have found that my days are somehow different when I call out for his help and expect him to be with me. All we need to do is to ask. God is near, here right now, with us.

* Matthew 10:29–31.
** Psalm 46:1.

After Trevor died, we had to move house. I prayed a lot for God's help and I was deeply touched by the practical care we received. We arrived to a garden so overgrown with brambles and ivy that the path was hidden, until a crowd of friends did a garden makeover worthy of a TV show, uncovering two hibiscus trees that give me joy every spring. The old shed was rotting and my friend Roddy set to it with a hammer only to speedily report back that it was beyond reclamation. My friend Ed 'just happened' to have a shed in his trailer which he and Roddy constructed for me that day. I share this because so often God shows his care for us through each other and maybe God wants to stir you to show someone else that they are not overlooked.

At different points when I felt most desolate, God showed that he was attentive to me. One tough week, I found myself vividly remembering how as a child, I had always wanted a hammock. I used to go to bed dreaming of where I would hang it! The next day, I prayed with the chaplain at the college where I work. She knew nothing about how this old childhood memory had just resurfaced and told me that she had a picture of God planting an uprooted plant in a hammock, where it would safely grow.

> I will be glad and rejoice in your love,
>> for you saw my affliction
>> and knew the anguish of my soul.

PSALM 31:7

ENGRAVED ON THE PALM OF HIS HANDS

God is eternally mindful of us. He never turns his eyes away. He reassures us with words, spoken first to his people, Israel, 'See I have engraved you on the palms of my hands.'*

* Isaiah 49:16.

Why would you engrave your hands? Just the thought of it makes me flinch. My friend Jake has the names of his four kids tattooed on his body. That is one devoted dad! What God has done shows a devotion far beyond that. God allowed the palms of his hands to be eternally pierced for me and for you. Jesus still carries those marks; they have not been erased from his resurrection body. They tell us how dearly we are loved.

In telling his people that they are engraved on the palms of his hands, God is saying, 'I don't forget you and I won't forget you.' Your name is not written on a sticky post-it note that will end up in the recycling. God has engraved your name on his hand. Write a reminder on your hand and it is there in front of you, all day, whatever you are doing. In telling us that we are engraved on his hand, God is saying that you are always before him – in his sight, on his mind. Right now. And forever.

Engraving is permanent. Couples engrave a wedding ring or carve their initials in a tree as a sign of covenant promise. It is even stronger than a tattoo. Johnny Depp had a tattoo that said, 'Winona forever'. Forever turned out to be rather brief and when his marriage to Winona Ryder broke up, he changed it to 'Wino forever'. Human 'forevers' never last forever and human covenants can fail. But God's forever is forever. You are engraved on the palm of his hand because he is eternally faithful to you and because he wants you forever.

God is eternally faithful to you and to me. The golden thread that runs through Scripture is the truth that God loves us with a forever-love. He says through his prophet Jeremiah: 'I have loved you with an everlasting love'.* God has always loved you, he loves you now and he will love you forever. This is the foundation of deep security.

When we grasp that God is eternally, lovingly mindful of us, we can risk anything for him. Mary, the mother of Jesus,

* Jeremiah 31:3.

understood this, singing, 'He has been mindful of the humble state of his servant.'* Could this be why Mary could trust God with her reputation and her future, because she knew that God was mindful of her?

EL ROI – THE GOD WHO SEES ME

This truth is so important for us that it is one of God's earliest self-revelations. As Scripture unfolds, we find that God has many names, each of which reveals a different part of his character. One of the earliest is *El Roi*, which means, 'the God who sees me'. To our surprise, that revelation was given to someone easy to overlook – a slave-girl and a foreigner, worth so little in her culture that she was used as a surrogate womb. Her name was Hagar. Her story is told in Genesis Chapter 16 and it is a shocker. Sarai, her owner, cannot have children and does not trust God enough to wait, so Hagar is farmed out like a prize cow to bear a child.

Why did Sarai take such a drastic step? She did not believe that God was mindful of her. Even though she had been promised children by God, she took matters into her own hands by involving Hagar. The longing for a child can be cruelly fierce and throughout Scripture, we see God's compassion to the barren woman so although the slavery remains abhorrent, we can understand a little of what drove Sarai. She faced not only her own natural longing for a child but the harsh voice of her culture which devalued the childless. At this point, Sarai was yet to learn to find her value through seeing the loving eyes of the One who sees us. She was probably terrified that she would be rejected as unworthy if she had no children. When we lose sight of the God who sees us, it is tempting to try and manufacture our own value.

* Luke 1:48.

Unsurprisingly, Sarai became jealous when Hagar got pregnant. That jealousy turned to rage when Hagar began to flaunt her growing belly and openly despised Sarai. Why did Hagar do that? Perhaps because Hagar too did not know that God saw her. We quickly fall into either rejection or pride when we think we are unseen.[*]

The story becomes increasingly ugly. Sarai responds to Hagar's boasting by turning to violence and starts to beat her. Hagar is left defenceless as her child's father, Abram,[**] steps back, failing to protect Hagar or his unborn child. Terrified, Hagar runs away. How desperate she must have been! She was a foreign, pregnant slave-girl in a desert campsite with nowhere to run. No women's refuge, no family, no friends. She was risking death for herself and her baby. Think of those refugees who cross deserts and oceans with their children; you only do that when you can see no other alternative.

With Gift of Blessing Trust, I once had a tour of the cells in a women's prison. A shockingly high percentage of women prisoners have experienced violent abuse at home. Some deliberately re-offend in order to get a prison sentence because even prison is better than home; at least they are safe at night. Hagar would have understood.

WHERE HAVE YOU COME FROM AND WHERE ARE YOU GOING?

Hagar flees across the hot sand, only to stumble across a spring of water, a well in the desert. In her misery, she finally cries out to God. She would have known about Abram's encounters with God and had heard enough about God to cry out to him. God heard her cry. He always does. Surely, it was God who directed her steps to the well.

---

[*] Genesis 16:13.
[**] Abram's name was changed to Abraham when God made a covenant with him (see Genesis 17:5).

There, a mysterious messenger from the Lord finds her and asks, 'Hagar, slave of Sarai, where have you come from, and where are you going?' It is not as if God did not know the answer. Sometimes, it takes us hearing his question to face not only our situation but to discover the truth that God knows all about it.

God knows where we have come from, all the failures and the mistakes, and he wants us to re-orient our lives back towards him, in the direction of eternity, and so he asks us, 'Where have you come from and where are you going?' Hagar replies by telling the truth, always a good plan with God. The Lord's response initially seems harsh; he does not allow her to run away. It seems that God rarely lifts us out of our circumstances; instead, he gives us strength to face them. For me, it was enormously stretching to go into a new workplace and a new church while vulnerable with grief, but, again and again, God stepped in to help. Sometimes, it was as I received loving prayer and sometimes as I prayed for others. I remember once standing awkwardly by the noticeboard at church, hoping that someone would come to talk to me. Then the Lord directed me to go and share a prophetic word with someone who had drifted into church. He ended up joining Alpha (a course for those exploring faith) and brought his family along. It is often when we are most broken that God steps in most wonderfully.

Hagar is told to go back to Abram and Sarai, perhaps ultimately for her safety as she would surely never have survived in the desert, but with this scary command comes a lavish promise of fruitfulness, 'I will increase your descendants so much that they will be too numerous to count.' Hagar, the rejected slave-girl, is given a promise that echoes the promise given to Abraham – a great lineage.

What comes next is astounding – Hagar is told God's name, 'The God Who Sees Me.' We might expect God to reveal his names to the great patriarch, Abraham, and he does so – in Genesis 14, Abram discovers that God is *El Elyon*, God most high, and in Genesis 17, Abram discovers that God is *El Shaddai*, God Almighty. But why did God choose to reveal his name, *El Roi* to Hagar who was not even part of his chosen people? If we see the big story of Scripture as the account of God's self-revelation, this is one of many surprises. In a culture which saw women and slaves as the lowest of the low, God chooses to reveal his character to Hagar.

Better still, this is no second-hand revelation. Clearly, Hagar had a personal encounter with God through this messenger. At first, we think it is an angel, but Hagar makes an astounding claim; she says that she has seen God, 'She gave this name to the LORD who spoke to her: 'You are the God who sees me,' for she said, 'I have now seen the One who sees me.'

In Hagar, God chose the most unlikely person for this revelation. Now, none of us need ever disqualify ourselves from this truth: 'God sees me'. Hagar's story tells us that our past, our gender, our status and our nationality are irrelevant. We do not need to be clever or important or accepted. All we need to do is cry out to God. We need never fear that God will overlook us. Our God is *El Roi*.

WHEN IT SEEMS THAT GOD'S EYES ARE SHUT

When Hagar was feeling another blow from Sarai, did she think that God was looking away? Did she think she was forgotten, like the Psalmist in Psalm 10? He cries out, 'Why, Lord, do you stand far off? Why do you hide yourself in times of trouble?'

There are times when it seems that God overlooks us but that is a lie. God may not act instantly but he never stops watching over us. The Psalmist eventually remembers that and points out that it is the wicked who say to themselves, 'God will never notice; he covers his face and never sees.'

After Trevor died, I wrestled with wondering if I should have spotted that he was ill. Did I miss something? Did I not watch closely enough? It is a familiar feeling for many who are suddenly bereaved. You trace over every moment to see if you could have done something to prevent it and regrets can overwhelm you. It has helped me that God has reassured me that he was watching over the moment that Trevor ran out of this life and into glory. His eyes were not shut.

We do not know what the Psalmist was suffering but it seems that his cry was not just for himself. In his cry is our cry for all who are afflicted – the hungry, the enslaved and the refugee. This is our cry for the millions who face institutional injustice. As he prays, he remembers who God is – the God who sees us,

> *You, God, see the trouble of the afflicted;*
> *you consider their grief and take it in hand.*

PSALM 10:14

Our God sees all the trouble and grief in our world. God has considered it and God has acted. On the cross, God took it in hand. Today, God sees trouble and grief and he sends us to take it in hand, even if it means getting those hands dirty. We do so, filled with hope, because the day is coming when the God who sees all will finally end all trouble and grief forever.

LOVE ALWAYS SEES WITH EYES OF HOPE

Love ... always hopes ...

1 CORINTHIANS 13:6–7

How did Hagar feel when she first realized that God saw her? Did she realize that God had seen her being mistreated as a slave? Did she feel ashamed of how she had openly despised Sarai? It can be scary that our lowest moments as well as our flaws and failings are all glaringly visible to the all-seeing eyes of God.

Some years ago, I gave a talk on how God's mercy is greater than all else and found myself particularly praying for one of the organizers. Afterwards, we ended up in the coffee queue together and she broke down, saying, 'Kate, I'm not like these other "good" women here.' A past affair had filled her with such shame that she avoided coming to God. That day, she discovered that God forgave her and that he looked on her as a new creation, full of hope for the future.

The God who loves us, sees us with eternal hope. Hope saw the mother of a nation in a mistreated, runaway slave girl. Hope saw a mighty warrior in a terrified Gideon cowering in a pit. Hope saw a future king in a young shepherd called David. Hope looked at a blustering, blundering disciple called Simon and saw Peter, which means the rock. God sees us with hope and calls us to do the same for each other.

Have you ever dared to ask God how he sees you? We have found that one helpful way to pray for people is to begin by asking God this question, 'Father, how do you see this person?' On numerous occasions, God has given different people the same picture or verse for the person being prayed for. I remember when our children's worker, Sue, was prayed for like this by complete strangers who knew nothing of her role, and they saw her as a mother duck followed by a line of ducklings. She was deeply encouraged. One reason that I dared bring my first scribbled ideas into a book for publication was because someone who had no knowledge of my writing had a picture of me with a golden inkpot.

Asking for the Lord's view helps us to pray with hope. The church becomes the place where we see each other according to our destiny and not our history.

HERE I AM

When we grasp that God sees us with hope-filled love, we can lay down our masks. The psychologist, Dr Susan David, conducted a survey with over 70,000 people which showed that a third of us judge ourselves for having so-called 'bad emotions,' like sadness, anger or even grief. I wonder if the ratio of 'judgers' would be even higher for Christians? So, we hide our emotions and fix on our masks, not only with each other, but with God.

As for me, I have found these three words immensely helpful in my prayer life: *'HERE I AM!'* Only three words, but they pave the way for encounter with God. Abraham, Jacob, Moses, Samuel and Isaiah all said to God – 'Here I am' and the result changed them forever.

'Here I am.'

When I was overwhelmed by a tsunami of grief, God kept inviting me to say, 'Here I am … as I am.' Now, as I know more days of joy and peace, God still invites me to come to him as I am. We can be real with God because he knows it all anyhow. As the Psalmist says, 'You are familiar with all my ways.'* God wants us to offer him all that we are, no pretences, no defences.

What would stop us? Do we fear the judgment that Dr David talks about? Christians can mistakenly feel that we should have it 'all together', as if being sad is a lack of trust. The Psalms counter that; they do not try to be tidy – there is anger and fear and grief – all laid out before God with searing honesty. There is permission to lament. In a broken world, we need that. One of the most moving bereavement cards that we received simply said, 'We lament with you'.

God can handle our fiercest emotions. I remember one evening, early on after Trevor died when I was driving back home to an empty house and an empty fridge. I could not face ringing anyone; it is hard to disturb people on a Saturday night. I found myself utterly desolate as I drove towards the supermarket to buy a meal for one. It was easier to cry in the car because no one could hear. I yelled at God, blazingly angry about the prospect of going home to eat supper on my own. But as the storm died down, I felt uncomfortable

* Psalm 139:3.

about my rage. Should you talk to God like that? I wiped my eyes and turned into the supermarket carpark. Who should be there but one of my best friends. She was buying herself supper, so we pooled resources and had a special evening together. I have no question that God heard the raw, incoherent cry of my heart that night.

God does not want us to hide from him. This was sent to me by someone who had suffered abuse in her past,

> 'As one who has spent decades behind her various masks, I can testify to the grace of God who, when we find the courage to step toward him in faith, knowing we're at the end of ourselves, his loving arms wrap tightly round us, holding and protecting us, knowing our deepest hurts and fears, covering us so we not only endure, we heal, we grow and we become so much more than we'd ever believe we could be. All because at the cross our grief, anger, hurt are exchanged for mercy, grace and peace.'

We can dare to say 'Here I am' with God because God himself makes the offering of ourselves to him holy and acceptable.* He has made the way for us to say, 'Here I am' because he longs to say the same words back to us,

> *... you will cry for help, and he will say: 'Here am I'.*

ISAIAH 58:9

FREEDOM FROM PEOPLE-PLEASING

God's loving acceptance frees us from the crippling curse of people-pleasing. A recent study of 40,000 university students revealed that levels of perfectionism have significantly risen in that age group. The extent to which young people feel judged and try to appear perfect to secure approval has risen by 33%. Co-author of the report, Dr Andrew Hill, suggests that growing perfectionism may be a key

* Romans 12:1.

factor in the rise in mental health difficulties in this group.[48] It is deeply damaging when our self-image is based on how we perceive others see us. God designed us to make him our reference point.

At best, we lose courage when we live for the praise of others. At worst, we turn from God. Leading Pharisees believed in Jesus but refused to follow him because, 'they loved human praise more than praise from God.'* Many of us live life like that, before an imaginary jury box full of critics. I know of no cure for this people-pleasing disease but to consciously set the Lord before us and to find ourselves mirrored in his eyes of love. I wonder who is in your imaginary jury box? It changes everything when we know that the most important eyes of all are watching us with love.

Jesus began his ministry with the voice that said, 'You are my beloved son'. How much more do we need to live as those who are beloved and approved by God? Paul challenges us, 'Am I now trying to win the approval of human beings, or of God? Or am I trying to please people? If I were still trying to please people, I would not be a servant of Christ.'** It is only when we see the loving eyes of God that we are freed from people-pleasing. This is why the Puritans challenged each other to live before an 'audience of one'. If we are to be a prophetic church that dares to challenge the culture around us, there is no other way.

GOD'S HEART GOES OUT TO US

It was because Hagar encountered the God who sees and hears us that she could return to an incredibly tough situation. She was propelled back by God's promise that she would safely give birth to a son called Ishmael, which means 'God hears'.

* John 12:43.
** Galatians 1:10.

You shall name him Ishmael,
for the LORD *has heard of your misery.*

Our loving Lord hears our cries of pain. After Trevor died, there were moments when grief unexpectedly sledgehammered me from behind. Sitting on a train or walking down the road, I would suddenly find myself sobbing. Never once did anyone notice or at least show that they did. But God did. He saw. He heard.

God is eternally mindful of us. Luke describes this tender, compassionate, seeing love in his account of the widow whose only son had died.

> *Soon afterward Jesus went with his disciples to the village of Nain,*
> *and a large crowd followed him. A funeral procession was coming*
> *out as he approached the village gate. The young man who had died*
> *was a widow's only son, and a large crowd from the village was with*
> *her. When the Lord saw her, his heart overflowed with compassion.*
> *'Don't cry!' he said.*

LUKE 7:11–13 (NLT)

Despite the pressing crowd, Jesus saw this devastated widow and his heart went out to her. The Lord never sees us with indifference. If you are sorrowful, be comforted; God sees you and his heart goes out to you. This is the core of the gospel: God saw the misery of his world and his heart went out to us in Christ. God's heart hung on a cross for us.

RESURRECTION

If the story ended there, we would be left moved by the compassion of God, but grief would have the last word. But the story does not end there. The end of the story is resurrection.

Jesus walked over to the coffin and touched it, and the bearers stopped. 'Young man,' he said, 'I tell you, get up.' Then the dead boy sat up and began to talk! And Jesus gave him back to his mother.

LUKE 7:14–15 (NLT)

Around thirty years ago, I heard a sermon which summed up the gospel like this: we are drowning in a lake and God loves us so much that he jumps in and drowns with us. It is decades ago but I can still remember that it disturbed me sufficiently that I went to speak to the preacher after the service. He had rightly wanted to communicate that God suffers with us and indeed dies for us, but he had communicated that the God we know is a powerless God, able to empathize with us but ultimately unable to save us. At the end of his sermon, we had all drowned! It was as if he had never read the end of the story. He had missed out the best bit. He forgot the resurrection. It is so important that we know the end of our story.

With God, our story ends in resurrection. As the theologian, Jürgen Moltmann, writes, 'A theology of the Cross without the resurrection is hell itself.'[49] Because God is mindful of us, our story ends in new life. It did for Hagar, it did for the widow and it will for us.

A NEW WELL TO DRINK FROM

Hagar's story finishes with a beautiful detail. The well was renamed 'Beer Lahai Roi' which means 'Well of the Living One who sees me'. In a dry desert world that is overshadowed by death, we are invited to drink here often, at the well of the Living One who sees me.

REFLECT AND CONSIDER:

I lift up my eyes to the mountains –
*   where does my help come from?*
My help comes from the Lord,
*   the Maker of heaven and earth.*
He will not let your foot slip –
*   he who watches over you will not slumber;*

PSALM 121:1–3

Do I subconsciously expect God to ignore me? Or do I see him as the One who constantly watches over me with love?

When I am sad or grieving, do I know his heart goes out to me?

Do I look to God to help me? What can I ask him to help me with today?

Do I wear a mask with God? Can I say, 'Here I am'?

What might help me align my life towards pleasing God rather than people-pleasing?

How will I answer the question, 'Where have you come from and where are you going?'?

How does God see me?

Who does God want me to see with eyes of eternal hope?

A PRAYER

Father God, you know it all. Nothing can be hidden. So why do I act like a child playing hide and seek with their hands over their eyes, imagining they can't be seen? You see me and still you love me so I can confess my sins, share my hurts and hand over my fears to you. I can pour out the deepest longings of my heart knowing your heart goes out to me.

Here I am.

Thank you that you are eternally mindful of me today. Thank you that I can drink at the well of the living One who sees me.

Amen

Chapter 6

Forever My Father

*To all who did receive him, to those who believed in his name,
he gave the right to become children of God*
JOHN 1:12

*... we have never been absent from nor uncared for by Him ...
The best proof that He will never cease to love us lies in that He
never began.*
GEERHARDUS VOS[50]

As we begin this journey of knowing the God of forever, the starting place is the love of the Father for us. As we will see in the chapters ahead, the pictures of God that we carry in our hearts and minds determine how we approach him. We are invited to call God 'Father'. Jesus came to earth for this – to give us the right to become children of God. This is so important that it is fair to say that none of us truly know God until we can say with joy, 'You are my Father – forever.'

I have a friend who had such a difficult relationship with her dad that she avoids approaching God as her Heavenly Father. It might be tempting to skip this chapter if you feel like that but please linger here a while. What a waste it would be to live this life on earth as spiritual orphans when God wants to father us. If we sidestep the core biblical revelation that God wants to be our Father forever, we miss out drastically.

It is precisely because this revelation is so key that it is fiercely contested by Satan. In the same way that Satan questioned the sonship of Jesus, he constantly whispers to us, '*If* you are a child of God …' This is a fierce battleground because it shapes how we see God and ourselves. There is a reason that Jesus told us to begin our prayers with the word 'Father'.

Even Jesus needed this truth as the foundation of his ministry. Before Jesus had achieved anything of note on earth, God spoke over him from heaven, 'You are my beloved Son'.* If Jesus needed to hear those words as the foundation of his life and ministry, how much more do we? I need to come back again and again to hear my Father's voice saying, 'You are my beloved child'. I need reminding that this is my core identity. Daily, our souls need to wake up to who we truly are – much-loved children for all eternity.

In my lifetime, I have too regularly lived like an orphan and fallen for the lie that God does not care for me. My days are different when I trust in the Father's love.

My friend, Nico, posts umpteen gorgeous pictures of his kids on social media with the caption *#lovethisonealot*. I remember the first time that I saw that caption and sensed the Holy Spirit's prompt – 'that's what God says about you'. God looks at me and at you and says, 'I love this one a lot'. Just as Nico fills his home with pictures of his kids; God keeps you as the apple of his eye. He created you and rescued you for this reason – to make you his child forever.

We are invited to live every day as those who are deeply loved, who trust that the Father's loving embrace is at the end of life's journey. God has chosen us to belong to him not just for a week or two. We will be God's children forever. In a world so fragile that a microscopic virus can shake it, God's fatherly love is permanent, enduring as surely as his faithfulness – for eternity.

BECOMING GOD'S CHILD

It is because God so longed to father us that he made a way for us to be born again as his children, 'To all who did receive him, to those

* Mark 1:11 (ESV).

who believed in his name, he gave the right to become children of God.* However good or bad your natural genetic inheritance, here you are offered a new eternal identity. When you receive and trust in Christ, you are born again into a new family. As if that were not enough, not only are you born into God's family, you are also adopted into it! We doubly belong. Forever.

When we begin to glimpse how much and for how long our Heavenly Father has loved and will love us, it changes how we approach him and how we live. The joys of life become a gift from him. The challenges of life can be met with the knowledge that God is with us and for us.

For my boys, it changed how they grieved the loss of their dad whom they all loved so dearly. I am so grateful to Johnny and Connor who share their stories in this chapter and to Ben who shares later on. After Trevor died, Connor wrote,

> 'It was only 3 months since Dad had died unexpectedly when I was 20. I was at our student weekend away, and the talk was on God as a Father. After the talk, God reminded me of Psalm 51 which says that God won't despise a broken and contrite heart and I felt the Father saying to me, "It's ok for you to be broken before me". After this, I wept for a long time, but felt comforted that I could be honest with God. It was like the Father gave me a comforting hug.'

During that prayer time, someone gave Connor a picture of God the Father going running with him, just like Trevor used to do. As they prayed, the Holy Spirit came so powerfully on Connor that he had to lie down, overwhelmed by the love of God.

OUR FATHER

God longs to pour out his love into our hearts through his Holy Spirit so that we can know him as our Father through the good times and the hard times. That is why when Jesus was asked by his

* John 1:12.

disciples how to pray, he told them to begin with the word, 'Father'. Not 'Teacher', not 'Master', not even 'King' but 'Father'. We begin our prayer from the place of being loved.

If you have never before known God as your Father, then be encouraged because God the Son and God the Holy Spirit help us to know this in our inmost being. All of our dads are imperfect to different degrees but whatever our earthly fathers were like, God can re-father us. One of my greatest joys over the years has been seeing those who had a poor experience of an earthly dad begin to discover the lavish love of the Father. The great weight and life-changing power of the Trinity – Father, Son and Spirit – come to us to show us who the Father is.

THE SON REVEALS THE FATHER

It is striking that when Philip asked Jesus to show him the Father, Jesus replied, 'Anyone who has seen me has seen the Father!'[*] In essence, Jesus is saying, 'Look at me!' In his life on earth, Jesus modelled to us the qualities of a perfect father – loving, empowering, gentle, generous, encouraging, challenging, protecting, teaching, correcting, affirming and forgiving. That is why the prophet, Isaiah, could describe the coming Messiah, Jesus, as the Everlasting Father.

I know several people who found that Jesus was their way into knowing God as a father. My friend, Sue said to me,

> 'Growing up without a Dad (he left when I was about 4 years old), I found it difficult to understand God as Father and close to me all the time. And although I loved the idea of a loving faithful God, my only experience of a Dad was that he left.'

Experience of such abandonment can leave lacerating wounds, but Sue's story does not end there,

---

[*] John 14:8–9.

'*Through Alpha and Life groups, I began to know Jesus as my brother (I'd always wanted an older brother growing up as an only child). I could connect with the words of the song, "You're my friend and you are my brother even though you are a king". I recognised that God had been pursuing me and through Jesus showed me how he is a loving, faithful Father, my Papa ... and as I ran towards him, he ran towards me like in the story of the Prodigal Son and held me as that 4-year-old girl.*'

Look at Jesus welcoming the little children into his arms to give them a big hug and to bless them. Our Heavenly Father is like that – he never pushes you away.

Look at Jesus coming from heaven to earth to seek us out. God the Father could not be more different to the disinterested dad who cannot be bothered to engage.

Look at Jesus providing so much food for his hungry followers that there are leftovers, showing us that our Heavenly Father will provide more than enough.

Look at Jesus lovingly telling his disciples where they got it wrong, pointing us to the Father who lovingly disciplines his children.

Look at Jesus showing them new horizons, expecting great things from them – like walking on water and miracles! That is what a good father does.

Look at Jesus repeatedly reassuring us, 'Take heart' and 'Don't be afraid'. That is what your Heavenly Father does when you are afraid.

Look at Jesus forgiving Peter. God the Father always gives us a new start every time we come to him.

Look at Jesus protecting the adulterous woman from those sharp stones. Think of Jesus fighting our greatest enemy to rescue us. That is what our Heavenly Father is like, never hurting us, always protecting us, fighting for us.

The list could go on and on. Our view of our Heavenly Father does not have to be determined by our earthly one. Jesus shows us what the Father is like. If the very term 'father' is laden with unhelpful memories for you, then you might want to begin by calling God your Papa or your Daddy or your *Abba*. Invite God to renew your mind and show you what he is like. It is one of the great miracles that I have seen the Holy Spirit do again and again as he has done with Sue and with countless others.

Jesus told a story designed to shatter wrong ideas about what God the Father is like. It is found in Luke Chapter 15 and tells of two sons: a rebellious younger brother who gets lost far from home and an older brother who gets lost in jealousy at home. Their father lavishes love on both his sons. I used to think perhaps the father figure in the story was normal at the time of Jesus. Absolutely not! This story was shocking to the first hearers. The father would have been expected to reject his rebellious son, not to abandon his dignity by lifting up his robes to run to embrace the lad when he finally came to his senses and came home. In his book, *Jesus Through Middle Eastern Eyes*, Kenneth Bailey writes that Jesus, 'was not describing fathers as he knew them but rather creating a new image that he intended to use as a model for God.'[51]

Having experienced social distancing in the Covid-19 pandemic, I am glad that God is never socially distant! The parable of the lost sons in Luke 15 reveals that our God is a hugging Father. He throws his arms around his son and kisses him. That is what he does for us. We too can run into the Father's embrace and hear him joyfully say, 'This is my child who was lost but is now found!'

Jesus completely redefines our understanding of God as a father – both through this parable and through how he himself behaved. Perhaps because other nations called their gods, 'father', the Old Testament says relatively little about God being our Father, using the term only a dozen times. There are wonderful pointers like that in Psalm 103:13, which tells us that God is like a father who shows compassion to his children, but generally there is a wariness when it comes to addressing God as a father. The same fear is expressed in Islam that we might mistakenly think that God is like a flawed human father. But we can dismiss that fear because Jesus came in person to reveal our perfect Heavenly Father to us.

Jesus redraws our picture of fatherhood and then invites us into the relationship that he has with the Father. Luigi Gioia puts it beautifully,

> When it comes to the Our Father, we can only say it because Jesus said it first, and he is saying it still. Thus, if we want to understand the Our Father, if we want to go beneath the surface and understand why it is not just one prayer among many, but the very heart of the mystery of prayer, we must start by seeing what it means on Jesus' lips and what happens when he says it.[52]

Jesus was able to tell us and show us what God the Father is like because he knew God as his father. At his baptism, we are given a window into the tender heart of the Father for his son, 'This is my beloved son, with whom I am well pleased.'* And yet, not only a window but also a mirror – here is where we find ourselves – in the love in the Father's eyes.

> *No one has ever seen God, but the one and only Son, who is himself God and is in closest relationship with the Father, has made him known.*

> JOHN 1:18

---

* Matthew 3:17 (ESV).

The original Greek here describes Jesus as being so close to the Father that it is like 'a son on his father's lap.' God wants us that close. Could you dare believe that God wants you that close? As close and secure as a beloved child on his lap?

ABBA, FATHER

The Father calls Jesus his beloved and Jesus calls God his *Abba*, which is Aramaic for 'dear Father'. At the time, it was a word used by little children for their dads, but, unlike our word, 'Daddy', it is not a word that you grow out of. It is hard to translate because for us, 'Father' sounds distantly formal, like something out of *Downton Abbey*, while 'Daddy' sounds babyish. *Abba* is neither distant nor infantile; it expresses tender love combined with honour and obedience. That is the relationship that we are invited into.

Because we come from a culture of fractured families where obedience too quickly rings of oppression, it can be hard to grasp that the term *Abba* is inseparable from obedience. Yet *Abba* is the word used by Jesus when he faces the agonising choice as to whether to do what his father wants and go to the cross,

> 'Abba, Father,' he said, 'everything is possible for you. Take this cup from me. Yet not what I will, but what you will.'

MARK 14:36

Knowing and trusting God as your Abba is what enables us to do his will, even when it is costly, even when our sinful, fearful selves want to go another way. Obedience is never oppressive when it is held within loving trust. Imagine how different life could be if we continually trusted like little children who expect that daddy would never let them down. Daily, we can turn to our loving Father and expect him to be there for us.

In another eye-opening section, Kenneth Bailey describes teaching a group of village women in Lebanon about the Lord's Prayer. He was teaching in Arabic, explaining the Aramaic word *Abba*. The women were unusually restless, so he asked them what was going on and this is what happened next,

> One woman in the back shyly put up her hand and very gently told this poor foreigner, 'Dr Bailey, *abba* is the first word we teach our children.' On investigating, I found this to be true across Lebanon, Syria, Palestine and Jordan. These countries were once all Aramaic speaking, and this precious word has survived even though the language of the people is now Arabic.[53]

Abba is to be our first word as we come like a little child to the Creator of all.

It is wonderful beyond words that God the Father welcomes us to share the relationship that he has with his Son. For those of us who have struggled with feeling rejected, this invitation reassures us that we are included in the closest, most loving, most joyous relationship of the universe. Jesus wants us to experience the love that the Father has for him,

> *'I have made you known to them and will continue to make you known in order that the love you have for me may be in them and that I myself may be in them.'*

JOHN 17:26

The great sacrifice of the cross was for this – that the love of the Father for the Son might be ours.

> *See what great love the Father has lavished on us, that we should be called children of God! And that is what we are!*

1 JOHN 3:1

UNCONDITIONAL LOVE

My oldest son, Johnny gave a eulogy at Trevor's funeral that spoke of the extravagantly unconditional love of God. Trev would have been first to admit that he was a far from perfect dad, remembering those times that he got too cross with the boys when they were young, but precisely because he was so aware of his failings, unconditional love was hugely important to him. Here is part of what Johnny said,

'At the very heart of Christianity is a view of God as a good father. I have been reflecting on what that means since Dad died in October. I have a copy of Rembrandt's painting of the prodigal son in my bedroom. It depicts the young man in Jesus' story as dirty and yet enfolded in the love of his father. Dad's life showed me that I am never beyond the reach of grace because I have a heavenly father whose love is unconditional. That was the love that Dad knew, and it was the love which he shared.

'Shortly before I was born, Dad wrote of the love of God in his journal, "A God who enjoyed me even in my failure and immaturity because he saw the sincere intentions of my heart. A God I didn't have to strive to make happy, because he'd been happy with me the second I was born into his family."

'Dad was that type of father. I didn't have to strive to make him happy. Whether it was the day he gave me a hug after I failed my third driving test or the day that he attended a year 7 concert where my starring role was as "third percussionist" and I had a 182 bar-rest in a 200-bar piece of music. Dad had a diploma on the organ and had been a music teacher but as we were driving home, he celebrated my six bars of bell-bashing.

'I've always known that I was loved regardless of exam grades, sociability, or sporting success. I didn't have to strive to be loved. When I've piled unnecessary pressure on myself, Dad always said, "Don't stress, you're loved!"

'That love of my father helped point me to the radical, glorious, lavish love of God. Our Father God looks out each day to see if his *beloved child will run home. When he sees his beloved, dirtied and messy, he sprints and enfolds them in an embrace, whispering, "You are my beloved, I have known you and loved you since before you were born … my love is not conditional on your performance. Welcome home."'*

This is the mind-bending truth; we are outrageously loved.

GOD THE HOLY SPIRIT REVEALS GOD THE FATHER

As we have already seen from Sue's story, knowing the Father's love does not depend on having the perfect earthly dad. It is always a gift of God's Spirit and that means that it is on offer for all of us.

Many people live as Christians for years without the deep reassurance of knowing that they are God's beloved children. That was the case for Trevor who was a Christian for years before being filled with the Spirit and encountering the Father's love. A turning point for Trevor was after reading about David Watson, the church leader and evangelist, who was filled with the Holy Spirit when he simply asked and believed God had done it, rather than waiting for fireworks or emotions, trusting that what the Lord has said will be accomplished.*

Trevor was challenged to do the same. He went home to his room, shut the door, asked God to be filled with the Holy Spirit and then started thanking God that he keeps his promises. He wrote that initially nothing happened, but then came 'a great inner YES that I am a child of the King!'

Trevor found himself dancing for joy in his bedroom and at that time, he was definitely not the dancing type. Over the following years, God gave him an ever-deeper revelation of the Father's love and I watched Trevor's joy and security grow. After he died, a

* Luke 1:45.

repeated memory that people told me that they had of Trevor was how he used to stand on his tiptoes in worship, his arms flung up high, praising the Father who loved him so much.

The Holy Spirit is often called 'the Spirit of adoption' because he enables that 'inner Yes'. He brings that heart cry 'Abba! Father! Daddy!' out of the depths of our souls. We only have to ask God for the gift of his Spirit and he will reassure us deep within that we belong to God,

> For you did not receive the spirit of slavery to fall back into fear, but you have received the Spirit of adoption as sons, by whom we cry, 'Abba! Father!' The Spirit himself bears witness with our spirit that we are children of God,

ROMANS 8: 15–16 (ESV)

Johnny had a similar experience of that inner 'Abba! Father!' cry in 2012. He had been struggling as a teenager with anxiety and what happened was life-changing,

> 'One of my life's most profound spiritual experiences saw the Holy Spirit confirm my sonship in my heart. I can only describe it as my spirit and the Holy Spirit crying independent of my mind "Abba Father". I discovered what it means that "perfect love casts out fear". I had just come out of two years of intermittent anxiety. In that moment I knew that whatever the battles, my spirit can cry Abba Father – my life is in his hands.'

We can daily ask God to pour out his Spirit of adoption on us, trusting that this is God's desire. God longs for you to know that you can run into his throne room, knowing that you belong as a favoured son or daughter. God is always thrilled to see you when you turn to him. He says over you just as he spoke over his people, that you are 'the child in whom I delight'.*

* Jeremiah 31:20.

In his final evening on earth, Jesus said something quite extraordinary. He was praying to the Father about his disciples and he said that the Father loved them *as much* as the Father loved him.* Take a breath before you take that in. The Father loves you, his adopted child, as much as he loves his Son Jesus.

God loves you as much as he loves Jesus. Recently, Connor and I were watching BBC's *Race Across the World*, which follows various duos travelling hundreds of miles with limited money and no flights or phones. One of them was a mother and her adopted son. Halfway through the episode, the mother described seeing TV footage of a tsunami and imagining having to choose whether to let go of her adopted son or her natural son; she realized that she could not bear to let go of either of them. She loved her adopted son as much as her blood-related son. That is what God is like.

Henri Nouwen writes,

> I cannot fathom how all of God's children can be favourites. And still, they are. When I look from my place in the world into God's Kingdom, I quickly come to think of God as the keeper of some great celestial scoreboard, and I will always be afraid of not making the grade. But as soon as I look from God's welcoming home into the world, I discover that God loves with a divine love, a love that cedes to all women and men their uniqueness without ever comparing.[54]

LIVING AS BELOVED CHILDREN

Jesus promises, 'I will not leave you as orphans, I will come to you.'** The question is, 'Do we live as though we belong?'

Heidi Baker, the missionary who founded the humanitarian relief organisation, Iris Global, has cared for numerous orphans in Mozambique. In her book, *Compelled by Love*, Heidi describes how

* John 17:23.
** See John 14:15–18.

she would host sleepovers in her home, inviting eight of the children who had been with them for years and eight of the new children who had just been adopted. She writes, 'At first the new ones are so timid that they won't even eat anything from the fridge. They feel that they have to work for what they want – or they have to steal.' It takes a while before they realize that the fridge door is open to them![55]

Too often, I have come to God as if I did not belong, with little expectation that the fridge door is open. What about you? Do you know that you belong? Your adoption into God's family is part of God's eternal plan. Whether your parents wanted you or not, you were chosen in Christ to be adopted into God's family before the foundation of the world.* You have always been wanted and you always will be.

A while ago, I was leading a meeting and suddenly sensed that I had to speak on how God always wanted us. I had never done it before, but I asked everyone to turn to the person next to them and say, 'You were always wanted'. At the end, a man came up to me, tears in his eyes. After months of searching for his birth mother, he had finally met her that week only to find that she had lived an apparently happy life without him. His birth parents had never wanted him. But that night, God told him that he was always wanted.

God always wanted you and he always will. That makes you his cherished child instead of an accidental combination of cells. You belong. You are held in the eternity of God's desire for you. The One who says, 'I am the beginning' is your beginning. He planned you before you took a breath. He gave you that breath and he gives you eternal life.

Like the father in Luke 15, our Father says to us, 'My child, you are always with me.'

Now and forever.

---

* Ephesians 1:4 (ESV).

REFLECT AND CONSIDER

*See what great love the Father has lavished on us, that we should be
called children of God! And that is what we are!*

1 JOHN 3:1

Declare this verse over yourself, replacing 'us' and 'we' with your
name.

Do I live like I belong? Do I know that the fridge door is open?

Read the story of the two lost sons in Luke 15. Am I like the younger
son, lost far from home, or like the older son, lost at home? Or am
I safely home? Can I hear the Father say to me, 'My child, you are
always with me, and everything I have is yours'?

Quiet your heart and hear our Father say, 'You are my beloved child,
in you I am well pleased!'

A PRAYER

*Father God, thank you for the gift of your Holy Spirit of adoption.
Fill me today that I might cry 'Abba Father' from the depths of my
being. Thank you, my loving Father that you will never leave me as
an orphan. I am adopted as your own, forever welcomed home.*[56]

Amen

Chapter 7

Forever our Father

See what great love the Father has lavished on us, that we should
be called children of God! And that is what we are!
1 JOHN 3:1

There is an eternity of joy when I discover that God is *my* Father, but I still miss out if I stop there. God is not only *my* Father, God is *our* Father! That makes us eternal siblings! When we see that God has brought us into an eternal relationship with each other, with Jesus as our older brother, it transforms how we love one another.

We are always enriched when we realize that we are part of the most enormous family, God's family, and God is always much bigger than we expect. I remember the first time I visited the Congo – my brother was working there as a missionary – the church set up the most enormous welcome party, with dancing in the street. There were so many people there, the street was completely full, and it was an explosion of foot-tapping joy! Culturally, it could not have been more different to my upbringing, but there was my Jesus, spanning the continents! The gospel always bridges the gaps because God's embrace stretches infinitely further than ours.

Here is a glimpse of heaven because only together can we truly reflect God's glory. We are all made in his image but as individuals, each of us only reflect a tiny facet of the diamond splendour of God. God has planned it so that when we are together, more of his image is displayed. Only together as the Body of Christ can we display the love and grace and beauty of God to each other. We need to get in practice for eternity because this vision of every person, from every nationality and background worshipping God *together* is where we are all heading,

> *After this I looked, and there before me was a great multitude that no one could count, from every nation, tribe, people and language, standing before the throne and before the Lamb.*

REVELATION 7:9

There will be people from every nation in the world, and, just as at the very first Pentecost in Acts, we will be speaking many languages and yet understanding one another. That tells us that the very best of our different cultures will endure, yet instead of dividing us, we will be held together in the knowledge that we all belong to God.

Marie, who I mentioned earlier, told me how much it has helped her to see herself first and foremost as a daughter of her Heavenly Father. When I asked her what tribe she was from, Marie refused to say whether she was Tutsi or Hutu, because that division caused such horrific bloodshed. She said, 'I am not first Hutu or Tutsi or black or white, I am a child of God.' To be clear, it is not that God wants any of us to deny who we are; it is a joy to know that there will be different races and languages in heaven. But it is a gift for all of us to see that our primary identity is as children of the same Heavenly Father.

My friend Alwyn was a curate at our church in Richmond. His parents left Jamaica and came to England during the 1950s as part of the Windrush generation. He is black and my husband Trevor was white; I loved seeing the depth of their friendship which demolished boundaries and anticipated heaven. As Alwyn reminded us, this is an expression of our calling to live out on earth the reality that we are all children of God.

Here is a truth worth pondering: we are heading into eternity as one family. Why would we wait to start treating each other as beloved brothers and sisters? How can it be that racism still exists in our churches? How can we share the same Heavenly Father and yet treat each other so badly? Martin Luther King famously said, 'It is appalling that the most segregated hour of Christian America is 11 o'clock on Sunday morning'; over half a century later, apparently little has changed. Father, forgive us.

God's Church is designed to be a glorious display of unity that reaches across class and race and denomination; it is to be the place where everyone prefers one another in love because we are family forever. When heaven comes down, being white and western will no longer carry any weight or privilege. Our heavenly dad is neither white nor black nor British nor any other race. Can we let that truth plumb the deep places of our hearts where unconscious prejudice still grips us? Can we allow it to dismantle the pride in 'my way of doing things'? Can we let the vision of being one family, children of the same Heavenly Father, disturb us and inspire us until we refuse to be satisfied with bland, uniform churches that refuse to make the effort of crossing boundaries?

Reflecting on this with Alwyn has made it clear to me that we cannot passively accept the status quo. Achieving unity means change, not only from the bottom but at the top. Our unity must be reflected in our leadership, not just our membership. Without that, we are an amputated body and we will be unable to fulfil all that God calls us to do. Without both arms, how can we embrace the hurting and the hungry? Without both legs, how can we run after the lost?

I am absolutely convinced that when we are prepared to carry the cost (and it can be costly), to make the effort to reach out across race, class, educational ability or denomination, the blessing of God descends.

How good and pleasant it is
*   when God's people live together in unity!*

It is like precious oil poured on the head,
*   running down on the beard,*
running down on Aaron's beard,
*   down on the collar of his robe.*
It is as if the dew of Hermon
*   were falling on Mount Zion.*
For there the Lord *bestows his blessing,*
*   even life forevermore.*

PSALM 133:1–3

It is essential to make the effort to break down these barriers because it is here that God commands his blessing. Why would we ever want to miss that? I think of joint church prayer meetings that I have attended when God's presence was like fragrant, healing oil. God always shows up when his people stop building their own kingdoms and seek his. The very first Pentecost, the first outpouring of the Holy Spirit, happened when God's people, men *and* women, all united together 'with one accord',*

> *They agreed they were in this for good, completely together in prayer, the women included.*

ACTS 1:14 (MSG)

If we are those who long and pray for a fresh outpouring of the Spirit, our unity today is equally important. Unity has always mattered to God. Consider the great move of God's Spirit that began at Azusa Street in Los Angeles in 1906 and swept across the world. A terrible earthquake in San Francisco displaced over 300,000 people, leading to crowds from multiple denominations of 'Egyptians, Chinese, Indians, Mexicans and other nationalities' all worshipping together at Asuza Street Mission.[57] Sadly, that unity did not last but a spark was lit that spread across the world.

---

* Acts 1:14 (ESV).

In 1977, Father Raniero Cantalamessa was sent by the Vatican to a conference in Kansas City in the States. Of the 40,000 attending, around half were Catholics and half from other denominations. On the final day, the talk was on unity; it described the way that Christ's body, his church, was torn and split. The entire group knelt in repentance. Father Raniero looked across the venue and saw a big neon sign hanging over it with the words, 'JESUS IS LORD' and he grasped at a profound level that it is surrender to the Lordship of Christ that unites us.

His response was to humble himself and to ask a nearby Protestant Christian to pray for him to be filled with the Holy Spirit. The result was that Father Raniero had a profound encounter with the love of God and began to speak in tongues. From that time, the Bible came to life for him in new ways, and his preaching gained such vitality that he went on to become preacher to the Papal Household and to write books that have changed many lives. Father Raniero could have stayed in his corner. We all could. But we are called to step up, to reach out and to make *every effort* for unity.

> *Make every effort to keep the unity of the Spirit through the bond of peace. There is one body and one Spirit, just as you were called to one hope when you were called; one Lord, one faith, one baptism; one God and Father of all, who is over all and through all and in all.*

EPHESIANS 4:3–6

The word 'all' rings out from these verses; unity is where we are heading, so the God of all commands us not to settle into our entrenched positions but to exert ourselves for unity with all.

That may not mean agreement on every point; our unity is a gathering around our love for Jesus and our desire to share him. If we live with our eyes on eternity, we will so long to see others living for eternity that mission will be higher on the agenda than guarding my way of doing things. We may differ but we can honour one another in how we do it. Paul says,

Be devoted to one another in love. Honour one another above yourselves.

ROMANS 12:10

A brief look at social media quickly shows that our culture is not good at honour. The internet has released a flood of nastiness that would be unthinkable face to face. We are in a culture war that is increasingly polarized and it is urgent that Christians deliberately reach across political and generational divides. We are called to honour one another by listening with love, even when we disagree.

Nothing builds our unity like praying together. I cannot pray for you without loving you. During the coronavirus lockdown, I was one of many moved to tears as I saw churches unite together to fill the food banks and to pray for God's blessing over our troubled nation. Thousands of Christians from different races and denominations sang 'The Blessing' song, based on the shining blessing given by God in Numbers 6, the blessing that I love so dearly. I love the sign language version, which speaks straight to the heart and I was caught up in the joy of one version that includes my friend's son, Ollie, whose unselfconscious all-out worship has propelled others to Jesus for years. Whether you like to sing it as 'The Blessing' song[58] or the John Rutter version, or simply to say it aloud, this blessing carries the heart of God. It will have a mighty impact that so many have united to pray and sing these words over their homes, their streets, their cities and our world,

> 'The LORD bless you
>   and keep you;
> the LORD make his face shine on you
>   and be gracious to you;
> the LORD turn his face toward you
>   and give you peace.'

NUMBERS 6:24–26

It is when we receive and share God's blessing together that God writes his name across our lives for all to see.* Our unity is not an option. It is essential if we want people to know our Jesus. When we unite with God as our Father, we are living out heaven on earth.

By this, everyone will know that you are my disciples, if you love one another.

JOHN 13:35

CONFESSING AND FORGIVING ONE ANOTHER

Tragically, the history of the church is a history of division, not unity. At the heart of the 'Our Father' prayer is a line that challenges me every time that I pray it, 'Forgive us our sins as we forgive those who sin against us.'

We begin with asking God to reveal where we have hurt each other and him. It is significant that so many of the great revivals involved deep heart-searching and profound repentance. Confessing our sins to God and one another is an essential part of healing. This is not a one-off, it is the Christian lifestyle.

The same is true of forgiveness. If only we only needed to forgive once and never again! But because we live in a broken world with broken people in broken families, forgiveness has to be a way of life.

The church is like any family; most siblings squabble but squabbles can turn into wars. Hurts can cut deep and leave raw wounds. Without a prayerful commitment to forgiveness, there is no hope of us living out our calling to love one another as brothers and sisters.

How can we forgive? An eternal perspective makes all the difference. Because we know that our Heavenly Father will bring justice on the Day of Judgment, there is no need to demand our pound of flesh. Ultimately, all will be made right so we can lovingly

---

* Numbers 6:27.

stand for truth and justice without vindictively fighting for vengeance. Our Father will soon tenderly wipe every one of our tears away: why keep a record of the reason for each one? When we know that we will forever be children of the King of kings, even the biggest debts that we are owed look miniscule. For all eternity, we will be richer than we can dream of – rich in the love with which we are loved forever by our Heavenly Father – so we can let the debts go.

The God who crossed the ultimate divide helps us to do the same. Trevor grew up in the time of the 'Troubles' in Northern Ireland in the 1960s and 1970s and saw at first hand the power of prayer in bridging divisions between the Protestant and Catholic communities at war. Personally, he experienced the trauma of a bomb blowing up his dad's shop and causing severe injuries to a family friend, and it would have been easy to resort to hatred. He was deeply grateful that he was invited to join a cross-denominational group praying for unity in Northern Ireland and began to make friends across the divides. Trevor loved to tell the story of Gordon Wilson whose daughter Marie was killed by a bomb in Enniskillen, yet whose extraordinary response was to forgive the perpetrators and then to be involved in peace talks with paramilitaries from both sides of the conflict.

It is important to recognize that forgiveness does not mean pretending that everything is OK. It does not mean walking back into abusive relationships. Nor does it mean ignoring the criminal justice system and acting as if justice is irrelevant. What it means is daily forgiving those who sin against us and praying blessing over our enemies so that a bitter root does not grow up to strangle our faith and damage our church families. Again, the writer to the Hebrews tells us to make every effort towards unity,

> *Make every effort to live in peace with everyone and to be holy; without holiness no one will see the Lord. See to it that no one falls short of the grace of God and that no bitter root grows up to cause trouble and defile many.*

HEBREWS 12:14–15

Much as I have sometimes wished that forgiveness was an optional extra in the Christian life, it turns out that it is a command because forgiveness is part of the eternal nature of God. As his children, we are called to be like our eternally forgiving Heavenly Father. How could we imagine that we could hold hands forever with our Father God while refusing to hold hands with our brothers and sisters on earth?

Does that make forgiveness easy? I have found it the hardest of all the challenges that life has brought me. The deeper the hurt, the more costly the choice to forgive. Often it is a process, not the work of a moment. But always, God comes to help us when we ask.

It is only with God's help that Marie has been able to forgive. She tells me that forgiveness has brought her healing,

> 'Forgiveness is the hardest thing. But it gives the forgiver far more than it gives the forgiven. The first one to forgive is the strongest one. So, I feel that I am stronger for forgiving what happened to me and for what happened to all the people I loved and those who I did not know. The first to apologise is the bravest. The first to forgive is the strongest. The first to forget is the happiest.'

No one has ever asked for her forgiveness but she has recognized that the alternative is holding onto anger and pain,

> 'Losing my husband, losing my relatives – my grandad, my sister, my brother, my neighbours, my friends, the younger generations … I cannot shift those things from my heart. I can't remove those people. I can't just delete them; they are in my mind always. I can shroud them with forgiveness. I can forgive whoever caused it all. Unforgiveness did more harm to me than those who I had the power to forgive if I chose. When I felt angry, I wanted to harm myself. So, if you don't forgive, you are constantly drinking poison. Anger is something you've got to release, for your own mental health. To forgive is drinking wonderful, holy water.'

God loves each of us so much that he does not want us poisoned so he offers the healing holy water of forgiveness for us to drink.

LAVISH LOVE

The wonderful call to us to live as eternal siblings ultimately springs from the lavish love of God which is always reaching out to embrace all of his children. We cannot know God and refuse to love one another. Eternal life is knowledge of God and because God is love, knowledge of God is love. John writes, 'Whoever does not love does not know God, because God is love.'*

This love is more than warm feelings. It is as we actively love one another that we know God better. That is why my brother, Tim, found that one of his most profound encounters with God was visiting the slums of Kampala with a Ugandan church who care for the most desperately poor, providing mosquito nets and the gift of a future in helping school the children.

Knowing God involves the kind of sacrificial love that the early church showed. It takes effort but our faith is nothing without it,

> And we ought to lay down our lives for our brothers and sisters. If anyone has material possessions and sees a brother or sister in need but has no pity on them, how can the love of God be in that person?

1 JOHN 3:16–17

How can we claim to love God as our Father and not care for our brothers and sisters? How can we turn a blind eye to the systems of world debt that leave our brothers and sisters in poverty? How can we stay mute when the persecuted church suffer? How can we leave racism and unconscious bias unchallenged?

In Luke 10, an expert in the law asked Jesus how to get eternal life. As he so often did, Jesus batted the question back, asking the man how he interpreted God's law. The man answered,

* I John 4:8.

*'"Love the Lord your God with all your heart and with all your soul
and with all your strength and with all your mind"; and, "Love your
neighbour as yourself."'*

*'You have answered correctly,' Jesus replied. 'Do this and you
will live.'*

LUKE 10:27–28

Do this and you will live! Pour yourself out in love for God and
others and you will live – forever!

The gift of salvation is not to be tucked into a cupboard. It is a
lived-out knowing and sharing of God's love for us and through
us that will never end. It always begins with his love for us. Here is
where the divine circle of love is completed; the only way I can pour
out that love is by receiving it from God who loves us with a love
so lavish that when we receive it, it overflows to those around us.
Always, 'we love because he *first* loved us.'* That is the plan.

So, when our love runs dry, we can endlessly come back to the
One who is love. When our love is stretched, we can draw on the
ever-flowing source of his compassion and grace and when we give
that love away, heaven comes down.

* 1 John 4:19, my emphasis.

RESPONSE

Think of an aspect of another culture that inspires you or brings you joy.

Can you imagine what it will be like when every nation and language are worshipping together?

Is there an expression of church that is different to your own that you value?

Consider why God values unity so highly. In what ways have you acted for unity and in what ways could you?

Could you spend some time listening to someone who has suffered injustice because of their skin colour or their background?

What could you do to honour others who hold different views to you?

Is there someone that God is calling you to forgive?

If you recognize that your heart is hard, spend time repenting, asking God to give you a new heart, filled with His great love for you and for all his children.

THE PEACE PRAYER[59]

Lord, make me an instrument of your peace.
Where there is hatred, let me bring love.
Where there is offence, let me bring pardon.
Where there is discord, let me bring union.
Where there is error, let me bring truth.
Where there is doubt, let me bring faith.
Where there is despair, let me bring hope.
Where there is darkness, let me bring your light.
Where there is sadness, let me bring joy.
O Master, let me not seek as much
to be consoled as to console,
to be understood as to understand,
to be loved as to love,
for it is in giving that one receives,
it is in self-forgetting that one finds,
it is in pardoning that one is pardoned,
it is in dying that one is raised to eternal life.

Chapter 8

Shepherd of All My Days

*He is our God
and we are the people of his pasture,
the flock under his care.*

PSALM 95:7

The other day I picked up my mobile to send my son's new girlfriend a message on her birthday and accidentally sent a picture that said, 'Yo, little brother, happy birthday!' As I get older, my eyesight is declining at far too rapid a pace. With my tendency to mislay my glasses and then try to 'wing it', this has led to many embarrassing mistakes like this.

How much more dangerous is it if our vision of God is impaired! What if your view of God is clouded by your own bad experiences instead of being founded on truth? Some years ago, Stephen Fry said that the universe would be better off for banishing the god who 'is an evil, capricious, monstrous maniac.' I would want to banish that god too. But do we ask ourselves what our view of God is really based on? Where can we find a true picture of God? If we are to know our eternal God, we must see him rightly. The pictures of God that we carry in our hearts and minds determine how we pray and how we live. For most of us that involves dismantling some false perceptions.

Our eternal God reveals himself to us by his Spirit and through his Word. Sometimes he uses stories and sometimes metaphors. God knows that he is infinitely bigger than we can understand, so he reveals himself to us in terms of objects that are familiar. He says that he is a door or a vine or a shepherd or a loaf of bread or a light in the dark. I have heard people say that we need new pictures and metaphors to tell us what God is like because the scriptural ones are outdated. That is misguided. By all means, let us find creative and contemporary ways to help people relate to God but if we cast aside the God-given ones, we end up with a god of our own making. We might have to work a bit harder to connect with the older biblical pictures, but it is worth the effort digging when there is gold to be found. Without that, our prayers and our songs and our thoughts are impoverished.

James Mays writes, 'A metaphor used for theological purposes is very serious business. It does not simply describe by comparison; it identifies by equation.'[60] This is important – it tells us that the pictures that we have of God are key to how we understand him and core to how we know him. It matters how we see God.

Consider the description of God as our Shepherd. Jesus told us a story about a shepherd to help us know what he is like. I have never met a shepherd and I would guess the same holds true for most of us, so this shepherd image could seem unfamiliar and inaccessible, difficult to understand, but stay with me, because here is a window through which we can see and know the eternal God.

God is eternally a shepherd. Throughout Scripture, he has consistently revealed himself as a shepherd. God has always had the character of a good shepherd and always will. The prophet Micah, tells us that the coming Messiah will be a shepherd,

> He will stand and shepherd his flock
> in the strength of the LORD,
> in the majesty of the name of the LORD his God.
> And they will live securely, for then his greatness
> will reach to the ends of the earth.

MICAH 5:4

The Bible finishes with the promise that we will know him as our Shepherd for all eternity,

For the Lamb on the throne
will be their Shepherd.
He will lead them to springs of life-giving water.

REVELATION 7:17 (NLT)

THE SHEPHERD WHO LOOKS FOR ME

What is God like? He is like this – a shepherd, seeking a lost sheep, full of heart-lifting, hilarious, contagious joy when he finds it.

Now the tax collectors and sinners were all gathering round to hear Jesus. But the Pharisees and the teachers of the law muttered, 'This man welcomes sinners and eats with them.'

Then Jesus told them this parable: 'Suppose one of you has a hundred sheep and loses one of them. Doesn't he leave the ninety-nine in the open country and go after the lost sheep until he finds it? And when he finds it, he joyfully puts it on his shoulders and goes home. Then he calls his friends and neighbours together and says, "Rejoice with me; I have found my lost sheep." I tell you that in the same way there will be more rejoicing in heaven over one sinner who repents than over ninety-nine righteous persons who do not need to repent.'

LUKE 15:1–7

The first hearers of the parable were Pharisees, and they knew their Scriptures. Their ears would have pricked up when they heard Jesus talk about a shepherd. It was a familiar picture of God for them. They knew that Jacob, the great patriarch of Israel and King David both spoke of God as 'my Shepherd'. They knew that a king was often described as being like a shepherd to the nation. They knew through the prophets that because king after king spectacularly messed up,

God promised to come and do a better job and come himself to be a shepherd leader to his people. Long before Jesus was born, God had spoken through the prophet Ezekiel, 'I myself will search for my sheep and look after them.'*

When you know Ezekiel's prophecy, you realize that when Jesus explains why he had dinner parties with sinners by telling a story of a shepherd hunting for lost sheep, Jesus is making a massive claim. He is claiming to be more than a mere rabbi; Jesus is claiming to be God, coming to look for his lost sheep, for you and me. Today God is still looking for us, calling for you and for me through this story that Jesus told. Will you listen for his voice?

Imagine the scene: the shepherd begins his evening count of the sheep, '1,2,3 … 99 – *Oh no! One is missing!*' To me, sheep all look the same, but this shepherd knows every one of his precious sheep individually and although it is the end of a long day, still he sets out. The terrain is rough and hard going. If you have ever clambered up a mountain through undergrowth, you will know that you end up scratched and exhausted. The shepherd scrambles up and down the hills, calling, calling, calling, refusing to rest until he finds his lost sheep.

Why does he bother? He still has ninety-nine. Why does the one matter? This story tells us that each one of us matters to God. As we have already discovered, our God picks us out in the crowd.

My kids used to like the *Where's Wally?* picture puzzle books and we would scour a crowd on the page to pick out Wally standing out in his striped tee-shirt. To God, you always stand out. God says,

'*I have called you by name; you are mine.*'

ISAIAH 43:1 (ESV)

One of my favourite books, one that I often return to, is Kenneth Bailey's, *The Good Shepherd* which has helped transform my view of God. In it, he relates a story from a shepherd from south-eastern

* Ezekiel 34:11.

Turkey who describes losing one goat from his herd at the foot of the mountain. For hours, he looked for her, climbing up and down, imitating her call, until finally, bleeding from the thorns, he said, 'we heard a faint call and to our unspeakable delight we found her.'[61]

That is what God is like – full of unspeakable delight when he finds us. Pause for a moment and take that in. That is how much he loves you. God is like that shepherd who is not content with the ninety-nine sheep that he has already got.

A friend of mine took her four kids and her nieces and nephews up onto Exmoor to go blackberry picking. At the end of the afternoon, all the children jumped back into the Land Rover and they drove home. She went to the kitchen, got supper and called the children and to her utter horror, she realized that they had left one of her nieces behind. How did my friend respond? Did she sit back, have a cup of tea and say, 'Well, the rest of the children are here. At least I've got most of them.'? NO! She leapt straight into action and called the police and set out on a search party because she loved that little girl (who was, happily, found safe and sound).

God is always seeking us out. In Christ, God went all the way to the cross, to take on himself our sin and shame, all that separates us from him. Being a shepherd in the time of Jesus was a dangerous job. There were bears and mountain lions. There was no option of calling 999 in an emergency. A bad shepherd would run away and leave the sheep to their fate. Jesus described a different kind of shepherd, the kind that would be willing to die for his sheep. We never have to question whether Jesus is in the good shepherd or bad shepherd category; he demonstrated his goodness when he hung on a cross for us.

Jesus is not like the paid labourer who runs for his life when he sees the wolf because he is just hired for the day and cares nothing for the sheep. Contrast that with the good shepherd who will fight for them and even die for them. Jesus says, 'I am the good shepherd. The good shepherd lays down his life for the sheep.'[*]

* John 10:11.

Our God is a good shepherd who lays down his life for love. Always, he is seeking you, always calling you home. Today, he calls your name, waiting for your answering cry to come and rescue you. That is true if you do not know him and true if you have been a Christian for years. I can still get in a tangle, like a sheep tangled in a thicket, but God always comes when I call out to him from the midst of my tangled thoughts or my tangled emotions or my tangled relationships. God is good at untangling each one of us. I am amazed at how often he answers that desperate 'arrow' prayer asking him to set us free. It may not always happen immediately, but God is an utterly reliable rescuer. King David understood this,

> *My eyes are ever on the* LORD,
> *for only he will release my feet from the snare.*

PSALM 25:15

OUR SHEPHERD UNTANGLES HIS SHEEP

I wonder do you know that he is listening today for your cry? Last year, I was speaking on this Shepherd passage at my church. Before I spoke, a student called Dan told his story. I knew that there had been a link between Dan and my son, Connor, but had never heard his full story and it was delightful timing that Dan, unbeknown to any of us, was to tell it on the very night I was preaching.

Dan grew up with a Christian background but threw it aside on coming to university. He started dabbling with drugs and got sucked in, to the point where he overdosed. He ended up in the resuscitation unit in A&E and there he prayed for God's help. He told the doctor that things needed to change and the doctor replied, 'What are you going to do?' Dan said, 'I need to come back to God!', to which the doctor replied that he was a Christian and prayed for him. God had speedily answered Dan's cry.

Nonetheless, the following week, Dan had another out-of-control drug trip, although this time he avoided hospital. On the bus, the next morning, he prayed desperately, asking God to intervene in his life. A few moments later, my son Connor, who had never met him before, felt prompted by God to tap him on the shoulder and tell him that God loved him. On that bus, Dan invited Jesus into his life. He then joined our church where he did an Alpha course to further explore the Christian faith. God heard Dan's cry and was so kind that he also let me, and Connor, know what had happened. What a good Shepherd we have!

THE SHEPHERD WHO CARRIES ME

And when he finds it, he joyfully puts it on his shoulders.

LUKE 15:5

What happens next? I guess that the sheep is exhausted after wandering lost for hours and is incapable of walking any further, so the shepherd hoists it up on his shoulders. Sheep are big; I was shocked to discover that a grown sheep with a fleece can weigh between 175lbs (80kgs) and 300lbs (135kgs).[62] If I had been the shepherd, I might have been tempted to think about mutton stew at this point but instead of being angry about carrying this smelly animal, our shepherd is so delighted to find it that he makes light of the burden. We are told that he *joyfully* puts it on his shoulders.

Our view of God is often so askew that we expect the shepherd to find the sheep, shout, 'you BAD sheep', throw a rope round its neck and drag it back across the hills. Instead, he carries the lost sheep home rejoicing. Spurgeon writes,

> Remember you have given Jesus great joy in his saving you. He was forever with the Father, eternally happy, infinitely glorious, as God

over all. Yet out of boundless love, he came, took upon himself our nature, and suffered in our stead to bring us back to holiness and God. 'He layeth it on his shoulders, rejoicing.' That day the shepherd knew but one joy. He had found his sheep, and the very pressure of it upon his shoulders made his heart light, for he knew by that sign that the object of his care was safe beyond all question.[63]

When God finds us, he picks us up and carries us. Isaiah tells us,

He tends his flock like a shepherd:
  He gathers the lambs in his arms
and carries them close to his heart;

ISAIAH 40:11

Oh, the tenderness of God! Isaiah dismantles our warped, harsh views of God and gives us a precious glimpse of his great compassion for us.

There is a reason that this was the main Christian picture for the first centuries of Christianity. Before the cross became the main Christian symbol, the picture of the Good Shepherd carrying the sheep was the image that filled the inner vision of the early Christians. This is the picture that we can still see on the walls of the ancient Catacombs of Rome.

Why was it so comforting to those early Christians who faced persecution? It was a visual reminder of the extraordinary combination of tenderness and strength that is the character of God. My friend James was a professional rugby player and describes playing rugby early on in his career for a team up in Newcastle. He told us that the strongest member of the team was a sheep farmer. Who needs weights in a gym when you can bench-press with a sheep?

Without a strong shepherd, sheep are defenceless. They are hardly fighting machines. No claws, no shell, no jagged incisors to rip into an attacker! In a land of bears and mountain lions, they relied on the shepherd to protect them. Imagine fighting a bear!

The shepherd boy, David, literally did. So, in Psalm 23, he describes God as the divine Shepherd who comforts his sheep with his staff and his rod. The staff had a hook on the end to pull a wandering sheep back into the flock. The rod was 2.5 metres long and studded with iron in order to beat off any predator. In Psalm 2, it is the mighty rod which will smash the rule of unjust dictators. We can know that we are ultimately secure when God is our Shepherd.

THE SHEPHERD WHO BRINGS ME HOME

And when he finds it, he joyfully puts it on his shoulders and goes home.

LUKE 15:5–6

Of all your friends and acquaintances, how many would you welcome to stay in your home forever? God brings us home.

Many people think being a Christian is about trying to be a good enough person to get into heaven. Our God brings sinners home. I love the description of Jesus that comes just before he tells the parable of the lost sheep in Luke 15. Luke writes, 'The Pharisees and the teachers of the law muttered, "This man welcomes sinners and eats with them."' In the original Greek, the religious leaders cannot bring themselves to utter the name of Jesus, leaving a blank, 'this … welcomes sinners and eats with them'. Why do they so hate Jesus eating with the so-called sinners? The Pharisees ate alone because they feared that other people's sin might make them impure. Here is Jesus inviting the lowest of the low – the sex-workers, the corrupt tax collectors and the thieves of the day – all are welcomed back home with him! Our Saviour has no fear that our sin will infect him. His holiness is infectious; he makes us pure instead of the other way around.

God welcomes us home to his table. In Psalm 23, God prepares a table for us; the implication is that there is a party already planned and that God is excited about hosting us. When my sons came home from university, we usually did a roast dinner or a curry take-out because we wanted to welcome them home. What a welcome God has ready for us!

WHAT PART DO WE HAVE TO PLAY?

When you read the story of the Good Shepherd, it might sound like God does everything and that we just wait to be rescued. But there is a part for us to play. Jesus finishes, 'I tell you that in the same way there will be more rejoicing in heaven over one sinner who repents than over ninety-nine righteous persons who do not need to repent.'

Our part is repentance. Consider for a moment, what does the word repentance bring to your mind? For many people, it sounds harsh, alienating and condemning. The biblical meaning could not be more different. It means turning around 180 degrees to walk in the opposite direction – into the arms of God. It is the decision to change the satnav from my own goals and to come home. Instead of living life for myself, I entrust it to the Shepherd and live for eternity.

I vividly remember the joy that filled me when Dan told his story. It is the same explosive joy that wells up every time I see a baptism. We are getting just a taster of heaven's joy. Every time we repent, whether for the first time or the fifty-first, all of heaven rejoices. Today, God is still rejoicing that you have chosen to turn to him. Our Shepherd is delighted to bring us home.

TRUSTING THE SHEPHERD TO PROVIDE

When I see that my God is the Shepherd who laid down his life for his sheep, I start trusting that he will always provide for all of my needs. He is the Shepherd of Psalm 23 who takes his sheep to good pasture, keeps them safe and makes them rest.

It is striking that so many of the great heroes of faith understood that lavish provision is central to the eternal character of God.

George Müller was one. He rescued and educated close to ten thousand orphans from poverty in Bristol before his death in 1898. Despite having no guaranteed source of income, he took in child after child because he trusted that the God who gave us his Son will never withhold what we need but will graciously give us all things along with Christ.*

There were many days when supplies ran low and money ran out. One day, the housemother of the orphanage told George that the children were up and dressed but there was nothing for breakfast. George asked her to take the 300 children into the dining room and to tell them to sit at the tables. He thanked God for the food and waited. Within minutes, a baker knocked on the door. He had woken in the night and decided to bake three batches of bread for the orphanage.

Soon, there was another knock at the door. The milkman's cart had broken down in front of the orphanage. He asked if they could use some free milk as it would spoil by the time the wheel was fixed. He brought in ten large cans of milk – enough for 300 thirsty children!

I was reminded of that story by my friend Alwyn, when he preached on it in Richmond. Alwyn not only preached about God's provision; he actually lives like he believes in it. Alwyn's life is a testimony to God's transforming power. He grew up in care, left school without qualifications and then went into the army where he joined the Army's airborne forces. When he left the army, he became a Christian, courageously went back to education, became a teacher and is now ordained. He personally discovered that God provides:

> *'Shortly after leaving the Army, I came to faith in Christ. I didn't have many transferable skills so my employment prospects were limited. I was offered a job in a warehouse nearby but financially, things were tight. I was paid weekly and by the time I had paid rent and bought food, there was little left. But I had recently discovered Jesus, and the joy of knowing him and being known and loved by Him was a great source of comfort and encouragement, as was my*

* Romans 8:32.

involvement with HTB (Holy Trinity Brompton Church) where I was worshipping at that time.

It was during a Sunday service there that I felt an inward nudge from the Holy Spirit, to put the contents of my pocket into the collection plate. In my pocket was a £10 note and a bit of loose change and it was all that I had left until the next pay day.'

Alwyn only had enough food to last the week but was reminded of Malachi 3:10 where God calls his people to give, promising, 'Test me in this … and see if I will not throw open the floodgates of heaven and pour out so much blessing that there will not be enough room to store it.' Alwyn put the tenner into the collection plate. He continues,

'As I did so, I remember praying something along the lines of "OK Lord, it's done, this is going to be interesting!" And for the remainder of the service, I didn't really think too much more about this.

'At the end of the service and as I was about to leave the church that evening, I felt a tap on my shoulder and a man was standing there and he said to me, "I feel the Lord is telling me to give you this." It was a £10 note. I was dumbfounded. I thanked him – and thinking that it was probably not appropriate to go into too much detail, I told him that his actions and kindness were a gift from the Lord.

'A few weeks later, the same thing happened again, on a Sunday evening. This time, I had £5 in my pocket, and under the same circumstances that I described earlier, I felt compelled to place the £5 note into the collection plate after which, I largely forgot about it. At the end of the service, as I was leaving the church I felt a hand on my arm, followed by a voice that said, "I hope you don't mind but I felt the Lord tell me that I should give this to you." It was a £5 note. Once again, I was blown away.'

When we know that God provides, we are freed to give. This is a way of living which leads to giving based on trust – the opposite of what Mark Sayers describes as the mentality of 'toxic entitlement' which pervades our culture.[64]

TRUSTING THE SHEPHERD TO LEAD US

We can trust God to provide for what is ahead. None of us know the way ahead but God does and we can trust him to lead us. The shepherds in the time of Jesus did not drive their flocks, they led them. They called the sheep and the sheep followed because they knew their shepherd's voice. Kenneth Bailey describes the way that each shepherd has its own unique call. If for some reason a sheep is moved to a new flock, when it is time to come out of the sheepfold, it will refuse to follow the new shepherd's call. It has the equivalent of a nervous breakdown and runs around banging its head on the stone walls. The sheep respond to their own shepherd.

God promises us that we will hear his voice as he leads us. Because he is God of eternity, we can trust that he knows the path ahead. Along the way, he will give us rest – the rest that our driven twenty-first century souls desperately need.

I am deeply moved that the last words of the patriarch, Jacob, contain the understanding that God had watched over him like a shepherd all his days. At this point, Jacob is described as being 'full of years.' That is not an exaggeration; he is 180 years old! His life has seen the devastating impact of his deceit and favouritism, of violence, fear, jealousy and grief. Yet this old man looks back to trace the hand of God on his life and is able to pronounce a blessing with great authority from, 'the God who has been my shepherd all my life long to this day.'[*]

Hundreds of years later, in the middle of the eighteenth century, another old man of faith knew the same God. As he looked back and forward, he wrote,

> Like sheep, we are weak, destitute, defenceless, prone to wander, unable to return, and always surrounded with wolves; but all is made up in the fulness, ability, wisdom, compassion, care, and faithfulness of our great Shepherd.

[*] Genesis 48:15 (ESV).

He guides, protects, feeds, heals, and restores, and will be our guide and our God even until death. Then He will meet us, receive us, and present us unto Himself, and we shall be near Him, and like Him, and with Him forever.[65]

Those words were written by John Newton who was once captain of a slave-ship. He had been responsible for unspeakable cruelty but after encountering Christ he penned one of the greatest hymns of all,

Amazing grace, how sweet the sound
    that saved a wretch like me.
I once was lost but now am found,
    was blind but now I see.[66]

I was initially horrified to discover that Newton wrote those words while still involved in slavery. But I think we can see Newton's life as a demonstration of the long-term transformation that comes with knowing God. It took years of following the Good Shepherd before Newton eventually took a staunch anti-slavery stance and became a significant campaigner for abolition. Over the years of knowing the Good Shepherd, he was led into paths of righteousness.

As I look back over both the joyous and hard moments of life, I can see that the Lord has been my Shepherd through it all, leading, caring, carrying, providing and protecting. What a privilege that we do not just call God the Shepherd; with David in Psalm 23, we can say, 'The Lord is *my* Shepherd.'

We can look ahead with trust, living and giving radically because we know that the great Shepherd of the sheep will lead us beside green pastures and life-giving springs of water through this life and into eternity and we will dwell in the house of the Lord forever.

RESPONSE

Is there one thing in this chapter that has changed your view of God?

Ask God where you are in the story of the lost sheep. Do you need untangling? Are you on the Shepherd's shoulders? Can you hear him rejoicing that he has found you? Can you trust him to lead you on the unknown paths ahead?

If you are a sheep, what do you need the Shepherd to do for you?

In what ways has God been the Shepherd of all your days?

Read Psalm 23 aloud once. Then choose one line to thank God for and one line to pray over someone else that you love.

Psalm 23

The Lord is my shepherd, I lack nothing.
He makes me lie down in green pastures,
he leads me beside quiet waters,
he refreshes my soul.
He guides me along the right paths
for his name's sake.
Even though I walk
through the darkest valley,
I will fear no evil,
for you are with me;
your rod and your staff,
they comfort me.

You prepare a table before me
in the presence of my enemies.
You anoint my head with oil;
my cup overflows.
Surely your goodness and love will follow me
all the days of my life,
and I will dwell in the house of the Lord
forever.

Chapter 9

Rock Eternal, King of Kings

Lead me to the Rock that is higher than I.
PSALM 61:2

As we continue our journey of knowing God, here is a revelation of the eternal God that will secure you.

He will be the sure foundation for your times,

ISAIAH 33:6

Ultimately all else crumbles but our God is a foundation of solid rock because our God is King of kings.

We all find our security in different places. Some of those go unnoticed until we lose them. My husband, Trevor, was like a rock in our family, utterly dependable and trustworthy and it was an enormous shock to us when he died. But not long afterwards, one of my sons said to me, 'Mum, I feel as if the little rock that we were on has crumbled, but we have landed on a much bigger rock.' He described it as being like discovering that you were standing on the enormous Ayers Rock that you see in pictures of Australia. He said, 'We are on a rock so broad that we can't possibly fall off it.'

God is the bigger rock. Isaiah says, 'Trust in the LORD forever, for the LORD, the LORD himself, is the Rock eternal.'* The Rock eternal is the sure foundation.

Does that truth mean that life will be predictable? Does that truth airlift us out of troubles or erase all our griefs? Not for my boys, nor for me. Yet God's love remains a sure foundation forever. It is not a plastic glib love that collapses in the face of pain. It is the love that is close to the broken-hearted.** Because of this love, God did not barricade himself away from pain but let his own heart, his own Son, be broken on the cross for us. This love is a sure foundation for all times – the joy-filled hours and the darkest of days. Other foundations fail but God is unchanging forever.

> You will keep in perfect peace
> > those whose minds are steadfast,
> because they trust in you.
> > Trust in the LORD forever,
> > for the LORD, the LORD himself, is the Rock eternal.

ISAIAH 26:3–4

How do we stay in perfect peace? By choosing to trust in God, the eternal Rock. I definitely cannot claim to live in a state of uninterrupted perfect peace, but I have known God steady me when I have trusted that my life is secure with him.

> My hope is built on nothing less
> Than Jesus' blood and righteousness;
> I dare not trust the sweetest frame
> But wholly lean on Jesus' Name.
>
> On Christ, the solid Rock, I stand;
> All other ground is sinking sand,

EDWARD MOTE (1834)

* Isaiah 26:4.
** Psalm 34:18.

Trusting that God is our eternal Rock holds us in the turbulence of life. It enables us to stand when the winds of our culture buffet us. Surely, this is why Isaiah and other prophets were able to speak out so bravely against the accepted standards of their day, challenging tyrants and foreign powers, facing beating and persecution.

CALLED TO BE COUNTER-CULTURAL

I have wondered how I would react to persecution for my faith and am challenged and encouraged by the example of the great Old Testament hero, Daniel, whose story is told in the Old Testament book named after him. As a young man, probably only a teenager, the terrifying foreign power of Babylon invaded his city, Jerusalem. In order to subdue the city, the King of Babylon took captive the brightest and best of the Israelite young men. Daniel fitted the bill, so he was taken into exile. He ended up miles away. The distance between Jerusalem and Babylon is around 2,700 km (around 1,700 miles) and there were no trains, no planes and no mobile phones to connect him with home or family.

The loss and disorientation must have been excruciating as Daniel found himself in a strange city with another language and different gods. Yet instead of desperately trying to fit in, Daniel stood out and kept his faith. He was secure on the Rock. Although he lived around 2,500 years ago, his life has much to speak to Christians who are in a minority in a secular culture.

Daniel was commanded to eat the court food which included items that were forbidden to God's people. It was no small thing for Daniel to refuse. At that time, Nebuchadnezzar was the tyrannical King of Babylon whose acts of cruelty included killing King Zedekiah's sons in front of him and then putting out his eyes. Understandably, Nebuchadnezzar's court officials did not want to upset him. When Daniel refused to eat the prescribed food, Ashpenaz, the official responsible for the exiles, said that he was far too afraid of his lord, the king, to allow Daniel to opt out of the court diet.

When you live in a free and democratic country, it is hard to imagine life in a repressive regime, constantly watched, fearing that if you step out of line, the consequences could be terminal. I was gripped by Sebastian Haffner's vivid account of life as a young man in Nazi Germany in the years leading up to the war.[67] He captures the atmosphere of terror. Those who stood out 'disappeared' and the majority were too scared to stand up to the mob rule that surrounded the Nazi regime. I suspect that level of intimidation pervaded the Babylon court in Daniel's day, yet Daniel's courage was outstanding. He refused to blend in. The Bible commentator, John Goldingay, explains that Daniel's refusal of the court diet was about 'avoiding assimilation'.[68] Daniel and his friends were prepared to carry the cost of being different. Their greatest aim was to honour God and to remain holy.

Daniel both unsettles and inspires. He is an outstanding example for us. One definition of being holy is being set apart for God. Daniel lived a life set apart. How does he do it? Every day, Daniel prays. There is no surer way to keep your life on the Rock, instead of being swept along by the current. He could so easily have responded to the official's fear by passively giving in. Instead, Daniel seeks God and is given captivating wisdom, responding by saying,

> 'Please test your servants for ten days: Give us nothing but vegetables to eat and water to drink. Then compare our appearance with that of the young men who eat the royal food, and treat your servants in accordance with what you see.'

DANIEL 1:12–13

In essence, Daniel is saying, 'Look, see if our diet works!' A few weeks later, Daniel and his friends are glowing with health. The official sees that Daniel and his friends are in such good shape that he allows them to stay on their vegetable-based diet.

It is rare to find people who dare to be different in the face of intimidation. Daniel stood up against the superpower of his day that looked undefeatable. He had been exiled to the most imposing city on earth. The fourth century BCE Greek historian, Herodotus, claimed, 'Babylon surpasses in wonder any city in the known world'. Its walls were close to 60 miles around, 300 feet high and a staggering 80 feet thick, wide enough for four chariots to race along the top.

Despite the awe-inspiring view in front of him, Daniel was more impressed by the invisible God. Those who are prepared to stand up and be counted always understand that the important and the immediate are different,

> So we fix our eyes not on what is seen, but on what is unseen, since what is seen is temporary, but what is unseen is eternal.

2 CORINTHIANS 4:18

The great reformer, William Wilberforce, wrote, 'The objects of the present life fill the human eye with a false magnification because of their immediacy.' After many years of effort, William Wilberforce was finally able to bring through a ground-breaking Act to abolish slavery in the British Parliament because he refused to accept the status quo in front of him. He saw through the illusion that the culture of the day was immovable. He saw the invisible. So did Daniel. That is why both men remained resolute.

Daniel saw the bigger Rock and so he continued to be fearless. He was eventually exalted to become an advisor to the king, one of Nebuchadnezzar's trusted wise men, but Daniel never forgot that his true king was *King of kings*. How quickly we forget that our God is King of kings. I can excuse myself by saying that it is because my culture does not acknowledge God. Neither did Daniel's. I can feel like I am in a minority. So was Daniel. Daniel was not swayed by his culture's judgment on God.

How did Daniel stay on the Rock? He stayed because he prayed. Daniel Chapter 2 tells us that Daniel stayed on the Rock even in the face of terror. King Nebuchadnezzar had a nightmare and decreed that all his wise men should be torn limb to limb if they could not explain it – an apparently impossible command since the king refused to tell them what he had dreamed! Knowing that King Nebuchadnezzar was quite capable of turning the threat into reality must have been petrifying but Daniel's response is to turn to prayer. He calls his friends to pray with him to 'the God of heaven', the one who is high above all. The result is that God mercifully reveals the king's dream to Daniel and Daniel is filled with praise for the King who is far above King Nebuchadnezzar,

> Praise be to the name of God for ever and ever;
> > wisdom and power are his.
> He changes times and seasons;
> > he deposes kings and raises up others.

DANIEL 2:20–21

Daniel sees that God is both king breaker and kingmaker because God is King of kings. Why should Daniel fear those whose days are numbered? Why should we?

It is not surprising that Nebuchadnezzar found his scary dream disturbing. It was of a huge statue with a head made of gold, the upper chest and arms of silver, the middle of bronze, the legs of iron and the feet of a mixture of iron and clay. A stone broke the feet to pieces and then the bronze and silver and gold were smashed to bits and blown away by the breeze until not a trace was left. Finally, the stone became a mountain and filled the earth.

What was the meaning of this weird dream? Daniel explains that each part of the statue was like a different kingdom. The head of gold was like Nebuchadnezzar himself, ruling over many nations. That initially sounds like good news for Nebuchadnezzar but then,

Daniel makes the shocking statement, '*After you,* another kingdom will arise'. 'After you!' – two words that put Nebuchadnezzar in his place; he will not endure. Nor will any other earthly kingdom. The different materials, gold, silver, bronze and iron and clay all represent kingdoms that will inevitably fall. The eternal Rock knocks them into oblivion.

History is strewn with the epitaphs of empires. Two years ago, I visited Rome with my son Johnny and was overwhelmed by the sense of power that still lingers on its streets. Everything towers. You could drive a bus through many of the doorways. Yet, Rome fell, just like Greece, just like every other empire including the British. The historian, Niall Ferguson, writes that Queen Victoria ruled an Empire that 'governed roughly a quarter of the world's population … and dominated nearly all its oceans' but that Empire, despite its arrogance, 'is long dead, only flotsam and jetsam now remain.'[69]

I remember the collapse of the Berlin wall. A friend, Bill Neely, was a journalist reporting that night. In 2014, he wrote for NBC describing it as the greatest story that he ever covered,

> Everything about the fall of the Berlin Wall was huge. The wall itself seemed immovable, a terrifying scar across a city divided between a pro-American West and a communist East. It was the line between nuclear enemies.
>
> It looked impregnable; the watchtowers and guards, the mines and moats, the dead ground and the hundreds of dead who had tried to breach it. But it wasn't. The political barrier – thrown up overnight on Aug. 13, 1961 – also fell in one night…
>
> … For those who grew up with the threat of nuclear annihilation, of 'mutually assured destruction,' Berlin was the center of the fear. The fall of the wall felt miraculous; it still does.[70]

Earthly kingdoms tumble. I wonder if the poet Shelley had Daniel in mind when he described the statue of the mighty and proud King Ozymandias lying in ruins in the desert. All that remains are the remnants of the legs and a broken part of the arrogant sneer on the face. Shelley warns us,

> Look on my Works, ye Mighty, and despair!
> Nothing beside remains. Round the decay
> Of that colossal Wreck, boundless and bare
> The lone and level sands stretch far away.[71]

Every idol ultimately tumbles and only God remains. The prophet Jeremiah tells us to look beyond the apparently impressive idols worshipped by those around us. He says, 'like a scarecrow in a cucumber field, their idols cannot speak.'* We must not be fooled by a scarecrow! The idols of our day are like the worthless wooden idols of Jeremiah's day that have been dressed up in blue and purple and gold and silver. We have to see past the dressing up. We refuse to bow down to the apparently impressive idols of physical beauty and money and fame and popularity and success and power that are worshipped all around us. Who will we worship?

> But the LORD is the true God;
> he is the living God, the eternal King

JEREMIAH 10:10

Every idol, every rock will ultimately crumble. Only that which is founded on God will remain. That is why Jesus told us the story of the crumbling house and the house on the rock.** One man built his home on the sand. Guess what happened when the first storm blew? How did he feel as he watched the walls crack? The other man built his home on the rock. Though the winds buffeted it and the waters rose, he stayed safe and warm.

We are left with the question – what will we build our lives upon?

---

* Jeremiah 10:5.
** Matthew 7:24–27.

STANDING FIRM YET NEVER DISENGAGING

What impresses me about Daniel is that he knew that the mighty walls of Babylon would collapse, and yet refused to disengage. He still learned the language and literature; he still prayed and worked for the welfare of the city. He lived out the call of the prophet Jeremiah to 'seek the peace and prosperity of the city to which I have carried you into exile.'*

In the 1960s, many Christians, including my parents, were warned against going to the cinema where they might become infected by its 'evil' and 'worldly' influence. They would now see that, by withdrawing, Christians then handed the big screen over to predominantly secular values. Throughout history, Christians have been tempted either to withdraw and 'stay pure' or to be carried along by the cultural current. Daniel presents the 21st century Western church with a mighty challenge. He engages with the culture and yet he stands apart from it. He is in the world but not of it.** I have heard sermons warning us not to be so heavenly minded that we are of no earthly use. If we are truly eternally minded, we *will* be of great earthly use. Every great prophet is eternally minded. They see beyond the present situation to what can be when God's kingdom comes, and believe that we are called to be part of the coming of that kingdom.

Precisely because we have a hope that is solid, we can be people of hope wherever we are placed. Our faith is more than pie in the sky because our God is an incarnate God who intervenes in the material world, who is above our culture and yet at work within it. We can pray and act with expectation. We are called to live with a solid hope based on the promises of God who loves us with a covenant love.

What a relief – we can take the focus off how trusting we are and place it on the trustworthiness of God. Our hope is not in our own

* Jeremiah 29:7.
** John 17:15–18.

ability but on the covenant love of God, on 'his faithfulness that vetoes our faithlessness.'[72] I have found that when my focus is on his purposes, life becomes exciting again.

SEEING GOD'S NEW THING

Has there ever been a move of God that happened without prophetic hope? Take the astonishing work of The Message Trust which has transformed countless young lives – it began when Andy and Simon Hawthorne felt a holy discontent about the state of young people in Manchester. Andy says,

> I read my set Bible reading for the day, Isaiah 43:18–21: 'Forget the former things; do not dwell on the past. See, I am doing a new thing!' ... I don't think there are actually any better or more relevant verses anywhere in the Bible that I could have read back then. They remain the touchstone words upon which everything we do is built ...[73]

Andy and his brother Simon began sharing Jesus with young people from deprived areas and that led to the formation of the World Wide Message Tribe band. Young people piled into music and dance events where they made commitments to follow Christ, but once these young people went home to troubled environments, it was too easy for them to tumble back into their old destructive lifestyles. Something radical was needed, another new thing. A vision was born that Christians would move into the poor areas and give themselves to see change from the inside out. They called it Eden.

> Central to Eden's ethos is the belief that in our participation in the transformation of a deprived neighbourhood, the best and most lasting change always comes from the inside out. This is how change comes in individual human life and it is how change comes to communities too.[74]

MATT WILSON

Dare we believe that broken communities can be changed? We must believe that or we will never act. Our church in Richmond partnered with St Peter's Church which borders Katanga slum in Kampala, working with the diocese of Kampala and with Karis Kids, which was started by my brother and his wife, Tim and Pippa Peppiatt, with the inspiration of Bishop Zac Niringiye. When I first visited the slum, I could not stop myself from retching as I walked past open muddy sewers. None of the homes have toilets and it is not safe for the women to come out at night, so they throw their excrement out in plastic bags. Large families live in a space the size of our sitting room. But we were utterly inspired by the determination of the church leaders there to bring change. For the cost of a meal out in the UK, families in our church were privileged to be able to contribute each month to help school children and to set up pathways out of poverty, which were laid by the phenomenal Ugandan team. I was moved to tears as I saw the impact of the Ugandan church during the Covid-19 crisis, feeding hundreds of children who would otherwise have died. They refuse to accept the unacceptable, seeing with God's eyes what can be.

What does it take to become those who engage with our culture and transform it with Jesus' values? It takes a belief that God can do a new thing, that mind-blowing transformation happens when people build their lives on Christ, the solid Rock. It takes looking beyond the present situation, looking beyond ourselves and crying out with the Psalmist,

> From the ends of the earth I call to you,
>   I call as my heart grows faint;
>   lead me to the rock that is higher than I.

PSALM 61:2

GOD'S KINGDOM IS COMING

What is the higher Rock? The kingdom of God! Knowing the eternal King is what makes our lives secure because his is the only kingdom that will endure,

> 'Holy, holy, holy is the Lord God, the Almighty –
> the one who always was, who is, and who is still to come.'

REVELATION 4:8 (NLT)

We will live differently when we see that the King is coming. When we see the devastation caused by Satan's rule, our heads droop and it is tempting to lose heart but as Rankin Wilbourne writes,

> 'It may not look like Christ is ruling the universe. Today it might look like just a crack of light under a door. But the New Testament writers were confident because they knew the light had dawned (Romans 13:12) and that one day the door will open, and that light, the Sun of Glory, will flood the whole room.
>
> The gravity of Christ being King is often lost on those of us who have no earthly king. But in the Roman Empire, the tiny church not only survived, but flourished, even amid terrible persecution.
>
> They were willing to die because they knew who the real king was. And they believed he was worth dying for.'[75]

It transforms how we live when we know who the real king is. There is a picture that sometimes fills my inner vision when I am worshipping. I see myself in an enemy-occupied city, like Paris in World War II, but the oppressors are even darker and crueller than the Nazis. In my picture, it is like the end of the war when the Allied troops came in and celebration and dancing filled the streets. I see King Jesus, glorious and beautiful, entering the city with his army, sweeping the evil regime away. I am in the crowds, cheering and cheering, bursting with joy because my King is here.

It changes this life when our eyes are on the day of the return of the King. We live and pray for that day when his kingdom comes – the kingdom of righteousness, joy and peace, the kingdom of solid rock, which sweeps all earthly kingdoms away.

RESPONSE

What have I built my life upon?

Are there areas of my life where I have been counter-cultural because I know God is my sure foundation?

What does it look like for me to be in the world but not of it?

What implications does it have for me that Christ will return as King of all?

As I look at our world with eyes of prophetic hope, is there a new thing that God wants me to do?

Spend some time simply repeating to God, 'You are my Rock'. Then think about what that means and add in another phrase that expresses what that means personally for you, like,

> *Thank you that you are my Rock, you won't ever let me down.*
> *Thank you that you are my Rock, I am secure.*
> *Thank you that you are my Rock, your reign will endure!*
> *Thank you that you are my Rock …*

You could do the same with the phrase, 'Thank you that you are my King …'

A PRAYER

Lord God, eternal Rock, may I live with my life founded on you. I am sorry for when I have not trusted you to be my Rock, for when I have tried to rule my own life. Today, I give myself to pray and live so that your kingdom comes on earth as in heaven.

Amen

Chapter 10

Behold the Lamb of God

'Worthy is the Lamb who was slain
to receive power and wealth and wisdom and strength
and honour and glory and praise!'
REVELATION 5:12

In this eternal adventure that is knowing God, here is an unexpected turn. God has not only revealed himself as Creator of time and space, not only as King of kings, not only as Shepherd, but as a lamb. On hearing that for the first time, it sounds bizarre! We might expect God to show himself as the Lion of Judah or a hurricane or an earthquake but how could the Almighty be like a little woolly lamb? Yet from beginning to end, throughout eternity, the identity of God is that of the Lamb.

Why a lamb? You could fill whole libraries with the answer because here are the depths of the love and greatness of God. My prayer is that as we linger here, the Holy Spirit will take us deeper.

John the Baptist introduces Jesus with words that ring across history,

'Behold the Lamb of God, who takes away the sin of the world!'

JOHN 1:29 (ESV)

Although the word 'behold' is old fashioned, it captures the sense that more than a cursory glance is called for. John is telling us not just to look, but to hold our gaze on the Lamb of God, to fix him in our sights, to keep looking until we begin to comprehend.

What did John the Baptist mean by calling Jesus the Lamb of God? Did John's first hearers begin to understand how important this was? Did John himself fully grasp the weight of it? In his notes on the Authorized Version, Bishop Westcott writes that it was 'a prophetic insight' given by the Holy Spirit.[76]

THE GREAT ESCAPE

For that very first audience listening to this strange locust-eating prophet, those words, 'Lamb of God' would have brought a rush of memories. I grew up watching the war film, *The Great Escape*, every Christmas, on our tiny black and white TV, following every twist in the plot, until it became so familiar that it held no surprises. Yet the following year, we happily watched it all over again. I would guess that many of us have cherished family memories based around favourite films that were watched over and over until we knew them verbatim and could quote them back to each other. In a far more profound way, the Israelites grew up hearing about their own Great Escape – from Egypt, and the central part that was played by a lamb, as they celebrated the Passover meal every year. Every year, each family would re-tell and share in the story of how Pharoah had stubbornly refused to release God's people from slavery despite warning after warning, despite plague after plague. Finally, the angel of death had swept through the city and every firstborn Egyptian son had died. God's people only escaped the deathly visit because each household had been instructed to bring a 'Passover offering' to God. They had to slaughter a lamb or a kid goat and to sprinkle its blood over the doorposts of every Israelite home, so that death would 'pass over' the homes of God's people.

The early church quickly came to see Jesus as their Passover lamb. Paul writes, 'Christ, our Passover lamb, has been sacrificed.'* They understood that Jesus was their Great Escape; he was the new Exodus! Now for us, Jesus is our escape from an even greater oppressor than Pharoah. His blood, shed for us, sets us free from slavery to sin, death and Satan.

I could tell countless stories of seeing Jesus set people free. Here is one from a beautiful and dear friend who has given me permission to share the freedom that Christ has won for her. This is a story of abuse and of rescue, and if this raises pain for you, I would encourage you to seek help. I have used a different name for her in this account.

Emily suffered the most horrendous abuse as a child. She grew up to be happily married and have children herself, but as an adult, eventually the memories were triggered, and she began to drink and self-harm to blot out the pain. She reached a point of breakdown and could not face leaving the house. I remember visiting and just praying in tongues over her as she lay on her sofa, barely able to talk. What happened next was a miracle as, over the coming days and weeks, Emily worshipped her way out of the pit of dark memories, out of captivity. One of her worst memories was that as a child, her cries had been silenced by a hand over her mouth, but now she is no longer silenced. Now she writes and sings worship songs that bring people into the presence of God. Here is what she wrote to me as she looked back to that dark time,

'At the time it just felt so hopeless, and it was that hopelessness looking back, that makes the deliverance all the more tangible. I had been drinking in secret for quite a long time when it got to the point of discovery. I was very good at hiding it. I had also been self-harming which was something I used to do as a child after each attack. The breaking point came when I cut so deep that I needed

* 1 Corinthians 5:7.

A&E treatment and then all my shame was laid bare and I had to admit to my husband and to myself just how low I had got. I could never explain in words the utter shame I felt that day in A&E, and also the desperate fear that I would have my children taken away. As well as handing over my bank cards and bottles that day, I also had to hand over the razors and knives that I had been hiding. I cannot begin to explain my hurt and shame.

'But I think for me what makes it so powerful and utterly amazing is what Jesus did next. I felt I was in such a low deep pit with no way out. I couldn't even speak let alone sing. Only the power of Jesus could have reached me in that place, only he could break the silence and lift the muzzle that I felt was not only over my mouth but my entire soul. I remember putting on Connor's worship CD and just sobbing. After some time, a song started to rise within me. Every battle I face from that day to this Jesus always says the same 'sing your way out!' And it always comes at a time when that is the absolute last thing I ever feel able to do, and it is always at the time when it is most powerful to do so.

'That day you and Trevor visited me I was so afraid. I felt sure that you would both be so cross with me – I was so cross with myself! I hardly dared to meet your gaze but I remember so clearly Trevor looking me in the eye with such love in his face and smiling at me. That was the love of Jesus right there. That gentle Lamb of God smiling at me through all the pain.

'I find now that Jesus has even healed me of the shame of those scars. I was so afraid of people noticing them, but actually, even this shame Jesus has now healed me from and I hardly notice my scars anymore.'

If you read this and recognize that you are in a pit of any kind, take time to behold the Lamb of God. Jesus looks at you with love in his eyes. There is help to be found, directly from God, from his people and from his provision in the form of the medical profession. God does not want you isolated and ashamed. With Jesus, there is freedom, and if the Son sets you free, you are free indeed! Jesus is our Great Escape.

THE POWER OF SACRIFICE

That escape came at great cost to God. To fully comprehend what it means that Jesus is the Lamb of God, we need to understand what it means that he was a sacrifice for us. From a twenty-first century viewpoint, a sacrifice seems primitive and bloodthirsty. Why was a sacrifice necessary? To begin with, the sacrificial system of the Old Testament helps to show us that sin matters. Our selfish acts cannot be dismissed as if nothing happened. Anyone who has suffered as a result of sinful behaviour understands that. Sin has a cost. The American theologian, Fleming Rutledge, explains why the sacrifice involves blood – it is because blood represents life, 'Blood represents the ultimate cost.'[77] An animal sacrifice tangibly shows us that sin needs recompense. Once the sacrifice has been made, it tangibly shows us that forgiveness has happened. As Rutledge goes on to write, 'In some sense, the sacrificial animal *takes the place of* the person who needs forgiveness…'[78] We can all see ourselves as the criminal, Barabbas, who is set free while Jesus hangs on the cross in his place.

It seems as if we are all wired to know the importance of self-sacrifice. Examine the great stories and you will find that self-sacrifice is a key thread. It is not just in the old myths. Look at Mr and Mrs Brown risking their lives for Paddington. Look at Frodo in *The Lord of the Rings*. Look at Lily Potter giving her life for Harry. Look at Iron Man sacrificing himself to save the Marvel Avengers' Universe. Look at the great war movies. We do not have to go back to ancient times to see the power of sacrifice.

It helps to see that the Old Testament sacrifices are more than a way to appease an angry deity. They are God's loving provision of grace for a wayward people to help them grasp that their sin has a cost. In providing the system of sacrifice in the Old Testament, God was making a way for his sinful people to come to him. It was always an incomplete system designed to point forward to the complete sacrifice that he had planned in giving us his only Son.

GOD HIMSELF PROVIDES THE LAMB

I have found it astonishing to see the many ways that the Old Testament prepares us to understand what God did on the cross. We can only skim over it here but take the story of Abraham and Isaac told in Genesis 22. Abraham waited a lifetime for a son and was so utterly overjoyed when the baby finally was born, that he named him Isaac, which means laughter. Then came the day when it looked as if laughter would forever be silenced. God asked Abraham to sacrifice his son. It is unthinkably shocking because God fiercely condemns child sacrifice elsewhere.* It can only be that God is using this story to test both Abraham and us in order to teach us, knowing that Abraham will never have to carry out this terrible command. From the start, Abraham himself trusts that he will not have to lose his son; he says to his servants, 'Stay here with the donkey while I and the boy go over there. We will worship and then *we* will come back to you.'** Abraham clearly expects that both he and Isaac will return.

To us, as we know the end of the story, Abraham's obedience looks hard enough, but how much harder must it have been for Abraham, who had to pack up the fire and the wood ready for the journey? Without arguing, Abraham trusts and obeys. Despite loving his son, a lifetime of trusting in our loving God has given Abraham mighty faith muscles.

As they climb the hill towards the place of sacrifice, Isaac asks his dad, 'The fire and wood are here ... but where is the lamb for the burnt offering?' Abraham replies in words that fly like an arrow to the cross, 'God himself will provide the lamb.'***

---

* Deuteronomy 12:31, Deuteronomy 18:10, Jeremiah 7:31, Ezekiel 20:31 and others.
** Genesis 22:5, my emphasis.
*** Genesis 22:7.

In the story of Abraham, that is what God did. At an agonisingly late moment, just as Abraham lifted the knife, God spoke, and there in the bushes was a ram.

In our story, that is what God has done. Although our sin is deserving of eternal separation from the Giver of Life, God himself has provided the sacrifice. God provided the Lamb. How can we ever thank him enough?

Surely he took up our pain
    and bore our suffering,
yet we considered him punished by God,
    stricken by him, and afflicted.
But he was pierced for our transgressions,
    he was crushed for our iniquities;
the punishment that brought us peace was on him,
    and by his wounds we are healed.
We all, like sheep, have gone astray,
    each of us has turned to our own way;
and the Lord *has laid on him*
    the iniquity of us all.

He was oppressed and afflicted,
    yet he did not open his mouth;
he was led like a lamb to the slaughter,
    and as a sheep before its shearers is silent,
    so he did not open his mouth.

ISAIAH 53:4–7

BEHOLD THE LAMB OF GOD

When we behold the Lamb, we see the love of Christ, who laid down his life for us. We see the love of the Father 'did not spare his own son but gave him up for us all'.* Because God gave up his Son for us, we know that God will never withhold any good thing from us.

When we behold the Lamb, we discover that the core of God's nature is self-giving love. We often use the word 'love' glibly, mostly to describe what we want to take. I love ice cream. I love my new scarf. I love my dog. This love of God is a different love, the love known in the New Testament as *agape* love, which is giving love. When we behold the Lamb, we see that God's love gives all; by the Spirit, Jesus gave himself and the Father gave up his beloved Son.

When we behold the Lamb, we know that God made provision for us from the start. The sin and suffering of our world did not catch God out. He provided the Lamb from before the world was made. You were redeemed, 'with the precious blood of Christ, a lamb without blemish or defect ... chosen before the creation of the world ...'.** As the biblical scholar, GB Caird, writes, 'Our redemption is part of the eternal order, planned before the creation of the world.'[79]

WASHED CLEAN FROM THE INSIDE OUT

When we behold the Lamb, we know that God has provided and that he will always provide. He has provided enough grace for you and for me, enough to cover *all* our sin. The Lamb is the sin-offering*** that we desperately need to approach our holy God. Unlike the Old Testament offerings that could only give an external ritual cleansing that enabled people to enter the temple, the blood of the Lamb of

* Romans 8:32.
** 1 Peter 1:19–20.
*** Isaiah 53:10.

God cleanses us deep within, removing the inner stain of guilt. We are made white as snow. For those of us who struggle with feeling condemned, this is inestimably precious. If the sin offerings of the Old Testament could provide ritual cleansing,

How much more, then, will the blood of Christ, who through the eternal Spirit offered Himself unblemished to God, cleanse our consciences from acts that lead to death, so that we may serve the living God!

HEBREWS 9:14

When my boys were younger they played football, and they used to go out with white shirts and return with very muddy brown ones. The only way to get rid of the stains was to soak them. How much more do we need to soak in the truth that the shed blood of the Lamb of God washes away the worst inner stains? The devotional writer, Andrew Murray, says, 'Conscience tells me what I must think of myself. The blood tells me what God thinks of me.'[80] God has provided the Lamb, so that we can boldly enter the Holy of Holies and meet with our God.

Recently, my friend Ellie was following the online posts of a shepherdess on social media. It happened to be the week leading up to Easter and she told me that she was profoundly affected by the account of adopting orphan lambs. Ellie wrote this to me,

'Do you know how orphaned lambs are adopted? Their legs are temporarily bound to stop them getting away, and they are brought to a birthing ewe. As her lamb is born, the orphan is immediately drenched in the birthing fluid of his new brother. It doesn't get much rawer than this. The blood and water are rubbed over the orphan so that the mother smells his scent on this forgotten creature and receives it as her own.

'When I come to my Father, might I remember that it isn't because he made some blasé decision to let me off the hook, because, somehow,

I've presented myself worthy or because God is "nice". No, I come because of the blood and the water poured out for me and over me.

'I get accepted. I am received. I am embraced as the Father's true offspring. Because I am hidden in the blood of the lamb, I receive all the love of the Father, and I always will. He sees me as he sees Jesus. He loves me in the same way he loves the lamb, his one true son.

'But where nature can never compare is that unlike the sheep who is somehow tricked into receiving new offspring, God makes the choice to receive us. No one tricks the Father into receiving us; God made a choice to sacrifice himself. I am chosen. You are chosen – all because of the love of the Father for you.'

As we behold the Lamb, we discover what God is like; we discover that loving self-sacrifice is at the heart of the character of God and so that is what we are called to. The persecuted church understands this. My friend, Eddie Lyle is President of Open Doors and has spent time with the underground church in China. I was deeply stirred when he told me that when they meet, they often ask the question, 'What scars have you borne for Jesus?' They have learned to follow the Lamb.

Eugene Peterson, who translated *The Message* version of the Bible, urges us not to seek power and follow the dragon pictured in Revelation. Instead we are to take the low farmyard route and follow the Lamb,

> worshipping the invisible … practicing a holy life that involves heroically difficult acts that no one will ever notice, in order to become, simply, our eternal selves in an eternal city.[81]

The way of the Lamb is the opposite to the way of sin and selfishness. Instead of demanding control and power, the Lamb is submissive. Instead of taking, the Lamb humbly offers himself.

Today, the Lamb comes alongside us still bearing wounds, the marks of love. He visits us in the breaking of the bread, in his broken body, that casts a bridge between us and eternity. Even exalted in heaven, he is still the Lamb who humbly gives away all for love.

AT THE HEART OF GOD IS SELF-GIVING LOVE

It is in the very nature of God
to offer God's self sacrificially.

FLEMING RUTLEDGE[82]

Right from the start, God gave himself to us. From before the world was made, God chose to sacrifice himself for love of us. He is 'the Lamb who was slain from the creation of the world.'* Jesus is unashamed of his scars – his risen body still had those wounds, which Thomas was invited to touch. Even in heaven, in all his glory, he still is the Lamb who was slain – those wounds glorified forever.

This means that we know that God is eternally self-giving. I might make the odd self-sacrificial gesture and then all too quickly go back to being selfish. God is not like that. God did not have a one-off moment of self-giving love on the cross; self-sacrificial love is who he is. In his deeply insightful book, *God With Us*, Rowan Williams explains, 'the cross is *not* an episode at the end of the life of Jesus but the coming to fulfilment of what that life has been about.'[83] To know the God of forever is to know the only person who *constantly and eternally* gives himself to us and for us.

From before creation, God planned to give himself to us.

Right now, God gives himself to us. He is the Lamb of God who offers us forgiveness today.

---

* Revelation 13:8.

Forever, God will give himself to us because he will *forever* be the Lamb on the throne.*

The Lamb is who God is for all eternity.

When I lose sight of God, I find him when I come back to the cross. More than ever, in the past years, where I could have felt abandoned and doubted the faithfulness of God, I have found that I can look to Jesus giving himself for me and know that the God who suffered for me, is always for me. The theologian, Jürgen Moltmann writes, 'The Cross on Golgotha has revealed the eternal heart of the Trinity.'[84]

STILL BEARING THE SCARS

That is why the risen Christ still bears the wounds of the cross in his resurrected body. Even in the book of Revelation, where the Lamb is the triumphant conqueror, he is still wounded. From the foundation of the world to the last day, from eternity to eternity, from beginning to end, Christ is the Lamb.[85]

Our God is not immune to suffering. He has not held himself apart, untouched by the pain in our world. When the Father saw his beloved Son sacrificed, he faced the fatherly agony that Abraham was spared. When the Son cried out that he was forsaken, Jesus came alongside every single one of us who has ever felt despair. Those wounds are now glorified forever and we need never feel alone when we suffer.

Behold the Lamb. Wait here a while, without rushing past Christ crucified. It is too easy to stroll past the cross like a familiar park bench because we have heard the story so often and we miss how outrageous it is that God should choose suffering for us.

Tom Holland, historian and author of *Dominion*, writes of how foolish the cross appeared to the first audiences,

* Revelation 7:17.

Nothing could have run more counter to the most profoundly held assumptions of Paul's contemporaries – Jews, or Greeks, or Romans. The notion that a god might have suffered torture and death on a cross was so shocking as to appear repulsive. Familiarity with the biblical narrative of the Crucifixion has dulled our sense of just how completely novel a deity Christ was. In the ancient world, it was the role of gods who laid claim to ruling the universe to uphold its order by inflicting punishment – not to suffer it themselves.[86]

Behold God suffering with us. Behold God suffering for us.

THE VICTORIOUS LAMB

I've read the end of the book and the Lamb wins.

SIMON PONSONBY[87]

Who would ever have imagined that from smallness, poverty, vulnerability and sacrifice would hide the greatest power of all? The final wonderful surprise is that it is the Lamb who is eternally victorious.

In Revelation 5, John weeps because no one is worthy to open up the scroll that contains all judgment, and the elders comfort him, saying, 'Behold, the Lion of the tribe of Judah'. John looks up and sees the Lamb. The Lamb and the Lion are one. The Lamb is the conquering Messiah who defeats the enemies of God. From beginning to end, this victory comes through sacrifice.

As Napoleon reportedly said,

Alexander, Caesar, Charlemagne, and I founded empires. But on what did we rest the creations of our genius? Upon sheer force. Jesus Christ alone founded his empire upon love; and at this hour millions of men will die for him.

If we follow Christ, then we too follow the way of the Lamb, the way of self-giving love. Our victory does not come through riches or weapons or force of character; we conquer sin and shame and fear and every assault of Satan through our testimony of Christ and by the blood of the Lamb.*

With all the saints throughout all the ages, we are to 'follow the Lamb wherever he goes.'** Too often, I want my own way, I want to be in the forefront, I want the praise, I want to be first, but the Lamb teaches me another way. He is led humbly to lay his life down, he is meek, he is obedient. Here is a victory that upsets every worldly standard. It tells us that rather than heading to a heaven where we accumulate more stuff, instead we are heading to an eternity where we will want to give ourselves away. Christ, the Lamb of God, shows us that the way to know God goes via the cross. The knowledge of God is cross-shaped.[88] So, with Paul, we pray, 'I want to know Christ – yes, to know the power of his resurrection and participation in his sufferings, becoming like him in his death.'***

Behold the Lamb of God.

REFLECT AND CONSIDER

'God is eternally self-giving'. Do you see God as holding back from you, or as endlessly giving himself away?

How does this example change how you live?

God promises to cleanse our consciences. How does this image help you?

* Revelation 12:11.
** Revelation 14:4.
*** Philippians 3:10.

When you see that God always planned to give himself as a sacrifice to redeem you, how does that affect the way that you value yourself?

> *For you know that it was not with perishable things such as silver or gold that you were redeemed from the empty way of life handed down to you from your forefathers, but with the precious blood of Christ, a lamb without blemish or defect. He was chosen before the creation of the world, but was revealed in these last times for your sake.*

1 PETER 1:18–20

Take some time to behold the Lamb of God. Behold, look, don't rush away – here is the love of God, all he gave that we might be saved. Set your gaze on the glory of grace.

A PRAYER

When I survey the wondrous cross
On which the Prince of glory died
My richest gain I count but loss
And pour contempt on all my pride
Forbid it, Lord, that I should boast
Save in the death of Christ my God
All the vain things that charm me most
I sacrifice them to His blood

See from his head, his hands, his feet
Sorrow and love flow mingled down
Did e'er such love and sorrow meet
Or thorns compose so rich a crown?
Were the whole realm of nature mine
That were an offering far too small
Love so amazing, so divine
Demands my soul, my life, my all!

ISAAC WATTS

Chapter 11

Maker and Re-maker

*Now the earth was formless and empty, darkness was over
the surface of the deep, and the Spirit of God was hovering
over the waters.*

GENESIS 1:2

In the beginning, the Spirit hovered. High over the darkness, far
above the chaos, tender above the deep, steady in the waiting, as
attentive as a new mother who cannot bear to leave her child, like a
bird hovering over its young. And out of chaos came creation.

In the beginning, the Spirit hovered. How long was it until God
spoke into the darkness and light cascaded? He said 'Let there be!'
and there was. From nothingness came craggy cliffs for us to climb,
honeysuckle scent and thunderous surf. From emptiness came a
star-strewn sky, molten rock, a dewdrop rainbow on a fragile blade
of grass and the unique whirls of your fingerprint.

Did God's creativity stop there? The character of God is that
he is Creator. God created the heavens and the earth but is still
creating and he always will be. God's Spirit is still looking for open
hearts, waiting to hover over our chaos and bring a new creation, to
remake and restore. That truth has been precious for me as I have
known God tenderly hover over the chaos of grief and bring a new
creation in our lives. It is part of the great Christian story that the
Holy Spirit creates beauty and order out of emptiness and loss. To
know God is to know the Creator.

The Holy Spirit is both described as being like a hovering dove but also as being like the wind or like breath. In Genesis 1, the word that we translate as Spirit is 'Ruach' which can also be translated as 'breath'. In the next chapter, we are told, 'The LORD God formed a man from the dust of the ground and breathed into his nostrils the breath of life, and the man became a living being.'*

God breathed his Spirit into us to make this stupendous spiral of DNA that is you and me, that intricate pattern of cells and sinews and longings and love and fingers and toes and grace and smiles and tears that he calls beloved.

Today, God wants to breathe his Spirit into our lives to make us anew. The God who created us is still at work creatively in our lives and always will be.

> Ruach, breath of God, breathe on me.
> You breathed dust to life,
> Ruach, breathe on me
> Jesus, you breathed like me till you were out of breath
> You breathed your last to give your breath to me
> So mine no longer is the end
> Ruach, hover over my chaos
> Breath of God, breathe on me.[89]

CREATOR OF ALL

When we begin to see that our God is Creator of all, the tiny boxes that cramp our faith are shattered and our expectation of what God can do in our lives is set free.

Our God is Creator of all. There is an old joke about a scientist who challenged God to a contest to make human beings out of dust. God replied, 'You're on!' The scientist went to gather a handful of dust, to which God replied, 'Make your own dust!'

* Genesis 2:7.

Our God is the Creator of all. That includes time itself. We must not imagine that eternity is bigger than the Everlasting God. God holds time and space in his hands. God contains eternity. My mind struggles to grasp that; this is how Reverend Dr Lincoln Harvey of St Mellitus College helps us understand it,

> 'The God of the gospel is eternal. This doesn't mean he is without time, but instead has the fullness of time. In his freedom, he is time's Lord and it cannot contain him because he outpaces it, embraces it. The past and the future are neither lost nor separated for God because he infinitely has the beginning, middle and end present to him as he transcends them through the eternal life of Father, Son and Spirit.'[90]

If that stretches your brain as it does mine, then let it inspire you to worship our infinite Creator God.

WE WORSHIP

How can we respond but with worship when we look beyond the gift of our world to the Giver? CS Lewis looks at the glimmers of glory that we see in creation and writes, 'One's mind runs back up the sunbeam to the sun.'[91] Instead of worshipping creation, we worship the Creator, joining the eternal song:

> *'You are worthy, our Lord and God,*
> *to receive glory and honour and power,*
> *for you created all things,*
> *and by your will they were created*
> *and have their being.'*

REVELATION 4:11

When we worship God as Creator of all, idols fall and fears flee. Our towering achievements and our greatest failures bow before the God of the galaxies.

With awe, Isaiah asks,

> *Who has measured the waters in the hollow of his hand,*
>> *or with the breadth of his hand marked off the heavens?*
> *Who has held the dust of the earth in a basket,*
>> *or weighed the mountains on the scales*
>> *and the hills in a balance?*

ISAIAH 40:12

Can you envisage God's hand marking off trillions of miles? Our gigantic sun is a speck in comparison. What should I fear when this is my God?

> *Do you not know?*
>> *Have you not heard?*
> *Has it not been told you from the beginning?*
>> *Have you not understood since the earth was founded?*
> *He sits enthroned above the circle of the earth,*
>> *and its people are like grasshoppers.*

ISAIAH 40:21–22

There is great comfort in seeing our smallness and God's greatness.

Before our Creator God, we fall to our knees. Our God is not a petty local deity, a tame pet or an idol to be manipulated.

> *'To whom will you compare me?*
>> *Or who is my equal?' says the Holy One.*
> *Lift up your eyes and look to the heavens:*
>> *Who created all these?*
> *He who brings out the starry host one by one*
>> *and calls forth each of them by name.*
> *Because of his great power and mighty strength,*
>> *not one of them is missing.*

Why do you complain, Jacob?
  Why do you say, Israel,
'My way is hidden from the LORD;
    my cause is disregarded by my God'?
Do you not know?
  Have you not heard?
The LORD is the everlasting God,
    the Creator of the ends of the earth.

ISAIAH 40:25–28

NO ACCIDENT

Without a Creator, the earth is spinning out to nowhere. 'Be who you want to be', 'I did it my way', from pop-culture to Disney, we have been told to self-create. Like the people of Babel, building bigger towers up in the sky, the West has replaced the Creator with a pale imitation. An increasing number paradoxically believe both the claim of new atheism that life has no meaning, and the claim of post-modernism that we all define our own meaning.

No wonder we are in the middle of an anxiety epidemic at the moment. This fragile post-Christian worldview contributes to the fact that 1 in 5 students and around 8 million across the nation are struggling with anxiety. There are multiple causes but surely a factor is loss of meaning, and the pressure to define your own.

When we lived in Richmond, a little charity called Kick London started out of our church; it was led by our friend Tom Rutter who wanted to reach kids through sport. Kick London has grown and now reaches about 10,000 kids a week including many who are marginalized and struggling. Joe Lowther, the inspirational CEO, told me about one 14-year-old pupil, who was described as having 'existential depression'. She saw no purpose to her existence and attempted suicide. She attended a church school, and a coach was mentoring her. In answer to her existential questions (and with the permission of the school) one day he shared what he believed. When she left the school, she wrote to the coach to thank him. She had been given a reason to live that day.

When we trust that God is our Creator, we can rest secure in the knowledge that our world was no accident. Our hearts lament over the brokenness of our world, but there is hope, because Almighty God created it by his good and perfect will and he has promised to restore it to his perfect plan – to unite all things in Christ.[*] God is patiently working that purpose out, seeking willing hearts that will turn to him.

CREATED WITH LOVE

The Bible reveals that God is like an artist who created us with great care. Each and every one of us can say, 'God is not only Creator; God is *my* Creator!' That changes both how we see ourselves and how we see God.

> For you created my inmost being;
>   you knit me together in my mother's womb.
> I praise you because I am fearfully and wonderfully made;

PSALM 139:13–14

You are not a rushed, last-minute school art project. God planned you before the universe was made. He knew about you before you were born. He created you with more delight than any human artist has ever had over their work. Many of us focus on our flaws; God sees the end design – he sees what he created you to be. That perfect design may have been warped and scratched but the Great Artist knows exactly how to restore it, because it is his original design.

[*] Ephesians 1:10.

That means that you are infinitely valuable. You never need to feel worthless because you were wonderfully made.

THE ETERNAL GOAL

When we see that God is by nature the eternal Creator, we can trust his creative work in our lives today. God created the universe from chaos into beauty and he has never stopped creating. The Creator made you with a purpose, with an eternal goal for your life and even if you have lost sight of it, he has not. Romans 8:29 tells us that God has called you and me for nothing less than this – 'to be conformed to the image of his Son'. The goal is to become like Christ.

In our self-willed, self-fulfilling culture, it is tempting to be enticed into the delusion that life is all about me. In the winter, we regularly watch the TV programme *Ski Sunday*, and I dream of being able to whizz down slopes with a panache that I will realistically never have. When I last watched it, it began with spectacular footage of skiers and snowboarders being dropped off a helicopter at the top of a mountain to ski off-piste on virgin snow. The voice-over pretty much summed up the ethos of our age, 'You do you! There's no right answer! There's no perfect line! Be who you want to be! Do what feels right!'

The tragedy is that being what we want to be is a descent to disaster. We were made to follow God's perfect line, to reflect the glory of God. The human story began with us being made in God's image, but we have smeared and smudged it. I remember a vivid illustration of this during the lockdown for coronavirus in the UK; the police wanted to discourage people from visiting local beauty spots so they deliberately ruined one of the most famous beautiful lakes in Derbyshire by pouring black dye into it. That blackened lake is what has happened to God's image in us. It is distorted and damaged because of our divided hearts.

God made us in his image, we spoiled it, but God still refused to give up on his goal for us. God in Christ came to restore all that was lost and that includes restoring God's image in us. God blesses us in order to write his character across our lives. Our story will end with his name written across our foreheads, with his likeness written across our lives.[*] That is what we were made for.

The good news is that God does not expect us to do this restoration work all by ourselves. There is a divine partnership with us. As we set our hearts to live out the great gift of salvation, God's mighty power works in us to fulfil his great plan for us – creating new hearts that want to go his way.[**] God himself is constantly working towards the long goal in our lives. Just before Paul tells us that God's purpose is that we should be conformed to the image of his Son, he writes, 'we know that in all things God works for the good of those who love him, who have been called according to his purpose.'[***] God's purpose is to make us Christlike.

BEAUTY FROM ASHES: TRANSFORMATION THROUGH SUFFERING

The God of always is always working creatively in our lives to restore all that was robbed. How is he doing that?

I remember someone giving that verse from Romans 8:28 to us shortly after Trevor died, with some comment about how our family must have needed this suffering to make us holy. Amongst the comments that we received, that was among the most tactless, and I remember it being the subject of some exasperated high-pitched discussion in our house. Thankfully, we have been on the road long enough to dismiss it as well-intended ineptness, but if

* See Luke 19:10; Revelation 22:4.
** Philippians 2:13.
*** Romans 8:28.

you know someone who is in the midst of grief, that is not what they need. It is generally best to just weep with them, pray for them, bring meals and love them.

Yet still, this verse has meant a huge amount to me. Because we were in the midst of a sermon series on being eternally minded just before his death, Trevor's final talk was on that exact verse. As a family, we have all listened to that talk a number of times and it has become a key verse for me. God made a good world and never intended any of the horrors or sorrows that it contains; instead God gave himself in Christ to defeat death and sin and Satan and all that destroys. And he will return to bring all suffering to an end. But for this short time, we still live in this broken world that Christ weeps over and it is here, in the midst of the very worst, that God works for our good. Here in the brokenness, God is working, recreating and restoring, in order to fulfil his great goal to make us like Christ. Because God's eternal plan is to restore his image in us, we can trust him to work in our lives through both the hard times and the good times to bring eternal transformation.

One of the best things about living in London is the free museums. A while ago, the Victoria and Albert Museum hosted an exhibition of jewellery that included some of the Crown Jewels and I was struck by the thought of the time and stress and pressure it would have taken to create every priceless piece. Who would have imagined that those glowing pearls were created by a horrid little irritant like a grain of sand? In order to protect itself from the irritation, the oyster covers the intruder with nacre – mother-of-pearl – until the precious pearl is formed. I could never have invented the story behind the sparkling diamonds which were formed around three billion years ago in the fiery depths of the earth. It takes the intense fiery heat and crushing pressure deep within the Earth's crust to cause carbon atoms to crystallize into the diamonds that can drill through concrete and celebrate enduring love. Even the gold of each intricate piece of jewellery was not the work of a moment; it had to be mined and refined in the fire before it could be carefully crafted.

The God who weeps with us in our pain also works, even in our toughest circumstances, to form his glorious image in our lives. I think most of us resist this truth because it is normal to avoid suffering, but it is noteworthy that when I ask people about the times their faith grew most, it is almost always during the storms. Sometimes, when I have spoken on suffering, I have asked people to raise a hand if their faith grew most in the tough times, and found that almost every hand is raised. If we trust ourselves to God when we go through the refiner's fire, our faith will be refined. As the American founder of the Vineyard movement, John Wimber, succinctly put it in a talk I heard some years ago, 'We grow bitter or better'.[92]

The great lie is that God has abandoned us when things are difficult. When life is tough, Satan whispers that God is finished with us, that he has abandoned his purposes for us. Nothing could be further from the truth. God says to his people,

> *Why do you complain, Jacob?*
> *Why do you say, Israel,*
> *'My way is hidden from the LORD;*
> *my cause is disregarded by my God'*
> *Do you not know?*
> *Have you not heard?*
> *The LORD is the everlasting God,*
> *the Creator of the ends of the earth.*

ISAIAH 40:27–28

God never gives up on us. He is both the founder and perfecter of our faith.[*] Right now, we can trust him to be at work in our lives, making us a new creation. We can refuse the lie that we are abandoned.

Paul refused that lie. Even though he had been beaten by his opponents and disappointed by Christians, shipwrecked and

---

* Hebrews 12:2 (ESV).

hungry, imprisoned and facing death, still he refused to believe that God had given up on him. He refused to believe that evil had won. He trusted in the God who works for good in all circumstances.

Most of us have dreams of our future, the way we imagine it will be, the good life ahead. I have found it helpful to see it like the picture on the jigsaw box of our lives. For us, when loss hit, it was as if the jigsaw that had begun to take shape was thrown up in the air and scattered. The losses kept coming as our lovely black Labrador got cancer and died, my friend Sonja died and I lost my beloved aunt. I had some continuity with my wonderful sons and wider family and friends but ended up living in a new home, with a new job and a new church and a new life.

When loss hits, our imagined picture on the box gets destroyed. We are left asking, can there be another picture or has the good life been lost? In my darker moments, I have asked, 'How can God turn my loss to good?' Since Trevor died, there have been bright shafts of light, grace-filled glimmers of redemption but at times, the cost seemed too big. I have had to trust that God has a picture for the box of my life that I cannot yet see.

After Trevor's death, I was greatly helped by Jerry Sittser's book, *A Grace Disguised*.[93] Jerry's wife, his daughter and his mother all died in a horrendous accident caused by a drunk driver. He vividly describes the devastation of grief and the bleak depression he suffered, never minimising his loss, but yet his book shines with love and hope. When asked if life can possibly be good again after bereavement, he describes the process of letting go of his old definition of 'a good life' only to find that over time, he has gained a rich life,

> What once seemed chaotic and random, like a deck of cards thrown into the air, has started to look like the plot of a wonderful story … The accident remains now, as it always has been, a horrible experience that did great damage to us and to so many others. It was and will remain a very bad chapter. But the whole of my life is becoming what appears to be a very good book.

Who else but our loving Saviour can take the fragments of our dreams, the pieces of our lives and make a new picture? Who else can turn all things to good? None of us can fully see the picture on the jigsaw box of our lives but when we trust that Jesus will be in it, we can trust that it will be good. The Creator who made the world and called it good is always at work for good in the lives of those who love him. He can even redeem the wrong choices, the wrong paths that we have taken, to make a new creation. Jesus said, 'My Father is always at his work to this very day, and I too am working.'*

What has this creative redemption looked like in our lives? I am very aware that I am still a work in progress and long to see more of God's image reflected in my life, so I am yet to see the full answer. But I can think of many ways that we have seen redemption and here are some of them.

To begin with, the last years have brought home to us that life is fleeting, and it is worth living with our hearts set on the eternal, not the temporal. Honestly, I do not always manage to keep that eternal perspective, but it has changed my priorities and freed me from being overwhelmed with the stress that came our way. I have had to step up and do things that I never expected, like buying a car and finding a new home, and it has made a great difference to my stress levels to remember that this is all small stuff in the context of eternity.

As I look back, there have been deep joys that have lit up the darkness of grief. God has given us the unexpected blessing of seeing people come to know Jesus. We have all seen people entrust their lives to Jesus as we have shared what we have experienced. I understand why many people perceive bereavement as abandonment by God and it has been a privilege to be able to speak of God's love to us in the midst of grief and then to see hearts and lives open up to God.

* John 5:17.

I have seen that God can touch the deepest and darkest places in my mind because when we cry out to God from the depths, we always meet him there. It is when our hearts are stripped bare before him that we are embraced by 'the God and Father of our Lord Jesus Christ ... who comforts us in all our troubles.'* Some of my deepest meetings with God have been in the midnight hours as I have wept with him. Over time, God has changed some of the darkest memories of that day that Trevor died. In the early months, I was unable to speak of it at all and then found that I could not speak of it without breaking down into tears. But God can even renew our memories. As I look back to that traumatic moment when I first saw Trevor in that ambulance, I can now see that God was there. Those darkest memories have been lit up by the glory of eternity. I would not have chosen this route for my life, but I am deeply grateful for how God's love has brought us through and changed the darkness to light, like a sunrise breaking over the crest of a hill.

It has then been a great blessing to me to discover that I am able to share that comfort with others; as Paul says, we 'comfort those in any trouble with the comfort we ourselves have received from God.'** Seeing others comforted because of what we have experienced is in itself a comfort that redeems the tears. For us as a family, we have been able to share at the deepest level with each other and that has been incredibly precious.

Our God creates beauty from ashes. His eternal Spirit hovers over the darkness to bring order and light and life. As we open our hearts to him, he makes all things new. I have been greatly helped by this picture of God hovering over me, spreading his wings over my heart, high above my bewildered grief, calling me to wait for his new creation. He is the eternal Creator who created the heavens and the earth, he is still creating, and he always will be.

* 2 Corinthians 1:3,4.
** 2 Corinthians 1:4.

LOOKING AHEAD

The end of the story is a new creation. We still have not seen the final masterpiece of the greatest artist of all. It is because God is the Creator that I am genuinely excited about what is to come after I die. In Chapter 1, I spoke of my childhood fear that eternal life would be boring. Not with the Creator, who constantly makes all things new! God will not suddenly stop creating when we get to heaven. It is his eternal nature and because we are made in his image, creativity is part of our nature too. Heaven will not be dull and static; it will be vibrant and life-giving. And because we are made in God's image, we will be creating too. The greatest adventure of all is yet to come!

RESPONSE

Say or sing these words out loud several times to God:

> 'You are worthy, our Lord and God,
>   to receive glory and honour and power,
> for you created all things,
>   and by your will they were created
>   and have their being.'

REVELATION 4:11

Then simply pray, again, several times, 'By your will, I was created'.

Consider the truth that you are 'wonderfully made' (Psalm 139). Does that change the value that you place on your life?

How do your life goals fit in with God's goal to make you Christlike?

Can you look back and see how hard times have brought transformation in your life?

Is there an area of loss or failure that you can bring to God, trusting him to turn it to good and make a new creation?

Knowing that you are made in God's image, how has he designed you to be creative?

A PRAYER

I worship you, my loving God, that you created all things. I praise you that you created me with love and so I am priceless in value. Today, you are still the Creator, restoring your image in my life. You will never stop working for my good until the day when all is remade. Come Holy Spirit, hover over all that is disordered and empty in my life. Breathe on me, breath of God and make me new.

Amen

Chapter 12

Buried Seeds, Deep Roots and Eternal Fruit

*Jesus knew that the Father had put all things under his power,
and that he had come from God and was returning to God; so he
got up from the meal, took off his outer clothing, and wrapped a
towel around his waist.*

JOHN 13:3–4

Do you remember that question that Hagar was asked, when the
Lord found her in the desert, running away from Sarai? He said,
'Where have you come from, and where are you going?'* Jesus knew
the answer to that question for his own life – he had come from God
and he was returning to God. He knew that he had infinite power.
And yet, what happens here completely shatters our expectations.
Powerful people normally expect special treatment – the highest
honour and the highest place. Jesus went in a completely unexpected
direction. He went low. He stripped off his outer clothing and
dressed like a slave in a towel. The King of kings knelt down and
washed grimy, smelly feet that had trodden with open sandals in the
dirt of the filthy streets.

Jesus knew where he had come from and where he was going.
So, he served. Here in these few verses in John 13 is a picture of the
whole gospel. Jesus took off the robes of majesty and stooped down

* Genesis 16:8.

low to serve us. Jesus was in very nature God, but did not grab at power or position for his own gain; instead, he emptied himself of self-promotion, 'taking the very nature of a servant, being made in human likeness.'* Jesus was so secure in his eternal identity that he was free to serve. He calls us to follow his example and do the same. He calls us to know our eternal identity and destiny, and to allow that to enable us to serve.

But so often, we find our identity elsewhere. At different times, I have put my identity in different things that made me feel important but none of them endured. I did fairly well academically at school, and in a culture where exams are important, it was tempting to find security in that. But the Bible says that knowledge will pass away,** which suggests that no one will be especially clever in heaven. That means that there is no point in putting your identity in what you know. The same goes for many other badges that we proudly wear. Over the years, I have spent far too much time worrying about what I look like but growing older punctures the illusion that appearance is everything. I realized the writing was on the wall when I spoke at a women's event and afterwards, I was given a gift of anti-wrinkle cream. I have gratefully used it while ruefully acknowledging that it is time to put my identity in Christ rather than how I look. If we are honest, most of us are tempted to define our value by temporary things, like our achievements or wealth or appearance or friends, but all of that is fragile – we cannot take it with us. God offers us an importance that is unrelated to these externals; it is that we are loved from eternity to eternity.

When we trust the eternal love of God for us, we are freed from the need to impress others, and we can give our lives to serve them. This is freedom. Imagine being so free from the need to look important that you kneel down in front of the people that you lead. That is what Jesus did. It was not merely an act to impress; God wanted to serve us.

* Philippians 2:7.
** 1 Corinthians 13:8.

We often look down on servants as being lower and poorer, as being somehow less than ourselves or others. Jesus shows us that we serve out of our richness. He served because he knew that God had put all things under his power, because he knew he came from the Father and that the Father held the future. It was because he knew that he was rich that he could give all. The same is true for us – we have Christ, so we are infinitely rich. I too often fall into a 'poverty mindset', one that fights for my position, but Jesus offers another way – the eternal way. When we see with an eternal perspective, we too can answer that question that Hagar was asked. We come from God's love and our loving Father holds the future, so we are utterly secure. So, we can give all. Dallas Willard writes,

> We know what is really happening, seeing it from the point of view of eternity. And we know that we will be taken care of, no matter what. We can be vulnerable because we are, in the end, simply invulnerable.[94]

When we see that our God is Alpha and Omega, Beginning and End we can say with the poet, George Herbert, 'I am but finite, yet thine infinitely',[95] and that sets us free to live radical lives of trust. Because the everlasting arms of God are underneath, holding us with love, we can dare to give ourselves away. Theologian Miroslav Volf puts it beautifully:

> A rich self looks toward the future with trust. It gives rather than holding things back in fear of coming out too short, because it believes God's promise that God will take care of it. Finite and endangered, a rich self still gives, because its life is 'hidden with Christ' in the infinite, unassailable, and utterly generous God, the Lord of the present, the past, and the future.[96]

THE GIFT OF SERVICE

We began this book with the call to reset the satnav of our lives. As we have seen, the eternal view resets our priorities. When we start to number our days here and see that what matters is knowing the eternal God, we will no longer live for ourselves but for him, sharing his love – for eternity.

Seeing the eternal perspective had that impact on my youngest son, Ben. He found the sudden death of his dad devastating, not only because they were so close, but because Ben had just started a university course, miles away from home. For Ben, it was a turning point, as he was faced with eternal realities. Part of his response was to commit to help cook breakfast for the homeless as part of a Christian student initiative called 'Just Love'. This is what Ben wrote for the 'Just Love' blog shortly after Trevor died:

> 'About a month ago I was sat in my new university room, coming to terms with a call from my mum that my dad had just died from a heart attack. I'm only a couple of months into my first term, so uni was an exciting new adventure and I can't say I thought about much else. But I was ripped out of it when I heard my dad died. I had never lost anything before him, and life was comfortable and safe. I took this for granted. But I was hit by life's frailty – our lives are but a breath (Psalm 39). As we drove home deep into the night, I thought with a new clarity and perspective – stripped to the core, rid of the fluff that I had made my identity. Never before had I so felt the need of my Saviour. If I truly believed in him then I needed to put him at the centre of my life.'

Ben went on to write that tasting both the bitterness of loss and the comfort of Jesus has given him a new determination to share God's love with others who face loss in different ways:

> 'The homeless have lost their homes and communities, the trafficked and the slaves have lost their freedom, hope, dignity and families. Just as Christ wept for Lazarus and for my dad, he also weeps for every one of these people, and he came to comfort those who mourn and to serve the poor.'

For each of us, the recognition of the brevity of life and the reality of eternity can sharpen our focus. You may not be called to serve the homeless, but God will have a unique part for you in serving him and bringing his love and justice in his world.

LOVING THE ONE IN FRONT OF US

So why do we often struggle to serve? I know that for me, my heart can be hard and proud, and I need to ask God to give me a new heart. But is it sometimes because we have been paralysed into inaction by the sheer enormity of the need? Our TV screens bombard us with pictures of suffering and loss until our defences go up. The onslaught of global tragedy is so depressing that we end up flicking channels and watching another box set.

How can we avoid being overwhelmed? Mother Teresa famously told us to begin by loving the one who is nearest. At the pool of Bethesda, Jesus was surrounded by sick people but healed the one in front of him.* We start by opening our eyes to the one in front of us. Jesus did not travel to every city in the world to supply every need. He went where the Father was calling him and did what the Father was doing. So too for us – God will have a specific part for each of us to play as we take the time to listen to him.

THE KINGDOM PRINCIPLE OF MULTIPLICATION

But really, can I make a difference? I am so small. What could I possibly do that will impact eternity?

In God's kingdom, the little can make a big difference. God does not despise the day of small things. With God, one man, Abraham, became a nation which has blessed the world.** With God, a pebble defeated a giant. With God, a child's picnic fed a crowd. With God,

* John 5:1–15.
** Zechariah 4:10; Genesis 12:2–3.

a handful of disciples became the church. With God, the little can be multiplied beyond all expectation.

Here is a new view of power. It is about offering the little we have to God. It is hard to take in because we are used to watching political power games. Having had three sons as teenagers means that I have watched most of the Marvel superhero films and spent more than a few hours watching evil villains who can pulverize planets being beaten to pulp by superheroes. That is what we expect of a kingdom – power with a punch! That is why so many countries keep trying to extend their missile ranges. That is why global military expenditure is a crazy $1.7 trillion, far more than enough to sort out world hunger, disease and sanitation.

Jesus came to bring a different kind of kingdom power. In Matthew's gospel, Jesus compares his kingdom to a seed. Bizarrely, in this case, it is a mustard seed. I find myself asking, 'Really?'. A mustard seed is about the size of a freckle. You could have one on your hand and not even see it. Yet Jesus said that his rule would not arrive with weapons and armies; it would be like planting a mustard seed.

It seems a strange choice because mustard trees are not particularly impressive plants. But something important happens in Jesus' parable; Jesus tells us that this mustard seed grows to a tree big enough for the birds to shelter in. I expect those first listeners would have immediately remembered that a tree where birds shelter was a picture of a mighty kingdom in Daniel Chapter 4. They would have known the promise of God's kingdom through Ezekiel who pictured a shoot which 'will produce branches and bear fruit and become a splendid cedar. Birds of every kind will nest in it; they will find shelter in the shade of its branches.'*

Jesus is telling us that this kingdom mustard seed will grow out of all proportion. It is extraordinary. How can a dot on your hand become like a towering cedar which can grow to a lofty 130 feet

---

* Ezekiel 17:23.

high? How can the all-powerful kingdom of God come from the tiniest, most insignificant seed? Jesus says that is how his kingdom works.

In case we missed the point, Jesus goes on to tell us that his kingdom is like planting a little yeast into dough and watching it balloon. In his parable, the dough grows to provide enough bread to make a hundred loaves! That is enough sandwiches to feed a huge crowd. Something tiny actively grows to create a kingdom feast. God has built a principle of mind-blowing growth into his universe – that is how his kingdom works.

Think for a moment about how you have seen this principle at work in your own life. Perhaps it is how you came to faith. I think of my friend Paula, whose amazing story of rescue is told in *The Promise of Blessing*. A loan of a tenner for her electricity meter, a prayer from a neighbour and some meals cooked when she was pregnant all helped bring her out of a destructive and addictive lifestyle to church and to Christ. Small acts led to immense change for her and to her family.

Apparently unimpressive people can have a huge impact if their lives are given to Jesus. One example is the relatively unknown Mr Nash (known as Bash), who was neither an academic nor an eloquent preacher, but he did care about sharing Jesus with teenagers. He spent his life sowing seeds of faith in British public schools and carefully nurturing young followers of Jesus at Christian camps. One of those was my dad who became a Christian through Bash's schools' ministry. As did the towering Christian leader and thinker, John Stott. The evangelist David Watson attended the camps, paving the way for his conversion to faith, alongside many others who have been influential in the growth of the church in the UK, including the Archbishop of Canterbury, Justin Welby.[97]

Canon David MacInnes, who was Rector of St Aldates in Oxford, came to faith through Bash and continued that pattern of liberally sowing seeds of the gospel, one of which landed in the life of Jackie

Pullinger (who led the miraculous work mentioned earlier among drug addicts in Hong Kong and has inspired many to see God's concern for the poor). David told me that Jackie had felt called to mission as a child, but her faith reawakened at a Bible study that he gave on Genesis. He chuckled as he remembered how crazy it was that this 22-year-old headed off to Hong Kong, which at first, she thought was in Africa. She bought a round-the-world ticket and jumped off the ship at Hong Kong and before long, she was praying for Triad gangsters and seeing them miraculously come off heroin without withdrawal symptoms. My brief time working with her was formative for me as it was for many others who are now leading in the church, including Heidi Baker and Pete Greig, founder of the wonderful 24-7 Prayer movement.

David MacInnes humbly and rightly insists that we all only play a part in what God is doing, often unaware of the impact that we have. I loved this encouragement, 'So many people feel inadequate when it comes to sharing faith, and have no idea of the way God uses almost throwaway comments to draw people in.' David is a great example because he fully expects God to use us and so is constantly and prayerfully sowing seeds which have amazingly multiplied. Another of the many seeds sown by David landed in the life of Nicky Gumbel who, in turn, has been influential in bringing so many to Christ through the Alpha Course. David described a priceless lunch where Nicky came to see him because he was worried that his friends, Nicky and Sila Lee, had joined a cult when they became Christians. Nicky read the gospels and encountered the risen Christ. Little seeds can have more impact than we imagine!

When we see that God's eternal kingdom on earth comes down to planting seeds, it changes your whole attitude to life and to doing God's work. The pressure is not on us. It is such a relief when you hear the truth – *it is not all about you*. When it comes to eternal fruit, we cannot create it. We just plant seeds. We cannot even make the rain to water them. Many of us believe the lie that I need huge faith or a big personality or a theology degree to see God's kingdom come. In fact, all we need is a very little faith – the size of a mustard seed.

The splendidly named Count Zinzendorf understood this. Yesterday as I was writing this chapter, I just happened to hear his story told by Pete Greig on the Lectio 365 prayer app. In 1716, when Count Zinzendorf was still a teenager, he gathered with some friends and founded the Order of the Mustard Seed. His inspirational story is too long to tell here but that seed eventually led to the first 24-7 prayer movement which lasted a century and to an explosion of worldwide mission. Zinzendorf influenced the Wesley brothers who in turn helped spark revival in Britain, transforming history and forming part of the stand against slavery. His life is still bearing fruit in the modern day 24-7 Prayer movement, not least through the Lectio 365 app. One life, one little seed – changing the world.

This is how the kingdom works. This is how the kingdom first came. God loved you and me so much that Christ laid down the majesty of heaven to become a seed, planted in a teenage womb, buried in a garden tomb, rising up to eternal glory. Jesus remains our example – as we give our lives away, they bear everlasting fruit.

DEEP ROOTS, ETERNAL FRUIT

God's plan for our lives always had eternity in mind. Jesus says to us, as he did to his disciples,

> 'You did not choose me, but I chose you and appointed you so that you might go and bear fruit – fruit that will last.'

JOHN 15:16

The plan is for us to bear everlasting fruit but there is only one way that can happen – when our lives are deeply rooted in the love of

God. In a storm-tossed wilderness world, we need deep roots if we are to bear eternal fruit.

When our family was hit by the storm of Trevor's death, a number of people reminded me of a tree in Richmond Park in London that he had mentioned in his sermons. I now have a photo of it in my sitting room and a stunning painting of it by Tamasin Warnock in my bedroom. You can see it on the Gift of Blessing Trust website, www.giftofblessingtrust.org, as it has helped form our vision.

In the UK, there was a great storm in 1987 in which a staggering 15 million trees were uprooted. Around 1,000 trees were toppled in Richmond Park. Yet some survived, those with deep hidden roots. The tree that Trevor loved was one of those. When it first fell, it looked devastated but it grew again to flourish and became an excellent picnic spot/pirate ship for my boys to climb on throughout their childhood. For us, it has been a promise that God can bring new life after grief as we root ourselves deeply in him.

When the roots are deep, a tree can survive and even thrive after a storm. We will only survive the storms of life and thrive if we set down deep roots into the love of God. As I look back, I can see that it is the knowledge of God's everlasting love that has held me through the desperately hard moments of the past few years. When we realize that we came from the Father's love and we are heading to it, grief is transformed by hope. Love is our beginning and our ending. And if God has our beginning and our ending, we can trust him with the middle, even the hard bits. The hard bits can be so painful but what a difference it makes when we know that we have been, are and will be loved by God forever.

God wants us not only to survive but to thrive and to live abundant lives that bear abundant fruit. That comes back to the refrain of this book – knowing God. Knowing God, knowing his love and eternal life cannot be separated. That is why Paul prays,

... I pray that you, being rooted and established in love, may have power, together with all the Lord's holy people, to grasp how wide and long and high and deep is the love of Christ ... that you may be filled to the measure of all the fullness of God.

EPHESIANS 3:17–19

No love could be wider – embracing you with open arms. No love could be longer – you were loved from the start and will be loved forever. No love has ever descended deeper – from heaven to the cross. No love could be higher – lifting us to heaven for all eternity. Today we are invited to root our lives in that love – until it fills us up with the fullness of God who is the source of both love and life.

ABUNDANT FRUIT

At Hampton Court Palace, there is the most famous grape vine in the world. It is 250 years old and was planted when Capability Brown was Head Gardener there. It is a mammoth 13 feet around the base and its roots stretch hundreds of feet underground towards the River Thames. The roots are so deep that it bears a huge crop. The average harvest is about 272 kilograms (600lbs), but it sometimes produces more than 2,000 bunches of grapes.

What would happen if I cut off one of the branches from the main vine and separated it from those deep roots? It would wither and die. Those branches are only fruitful because at every moment the sap, the life, is flowing into them from the vine. When you trusted your life to God, you were grafted into Christ, like a branch into a vine, so that every moment, the Holy Spirit, the life of God, can flow into you. Jesus says, 'If you remain in me and I in you, you will bear much fruit; apart from me you can do nothing.'*

* John 15:5.

The life and the fruitfulness both come from our connection with the eternal God, from abiding in his everlasting love. The eternal command is ultimately so simple, 'Now remain in my love'.*

This is how to live for eternity – today and every day for the rest of our days, drawing on and sharing the unfailing, never-ending, always-committed, self-giving, promised love of God for us.

TO CONSIDER

Spend some time thinking about what makes you feel secure. Are those things secure? Will they last? Thank God that there is utter security in knowing that you are loved from eternity to eternity.

How rich am I? Make a list of your riches in Christ.

Why do I struggle to serve?

Does inadequacy hold me back?

Can I remember a time when someone planted a mustard seed of the kingdom in my life?

What seeds have I sown?

Is there a mustard seed that I can offer to God today?

Read out the following, placing your name in the gaps: 'Jesus chose … and appointed … so that … might go and bear fruit – fruit that will last.' (From John 15:16.)

* John 15:9.

In a busy life with many demands, how will I set my life to know the God of forever and remain in his love?

A PRAYER

Father God, how can I ever thank you for your unfailing love? It is a priceless gift, given with nail-pierced hands. May I remain in your love today, receiving it and giving it away. May I receive it as I draw on the endless source of your loving Spirit. May I give it away liberally, little seed by little seed, that my life may bear everlasting fruit, for your glory.

Amen

Infinitely More

What a glorious future lies ahead, filled with the infinite joy of knowing the God of forever who has loved us from the start and will love us forever. Nothing compares to knowing God and nothing matters more. Here is eternal life. We never need to apologize for this message; this is what every soul in our unstable world desperately needs.

This book has focused on aspects of God's eternal character that have particularly blessed me but there is so much more to God. We have barely skimmed the surface. What about God the eternal lover of our souls, adoring his people like a bridegroom passionately in love with his new bride, eagerly anticipating the marriage feast that is ahead? What about the eternal cry, 'Holy, Holy, Holy'? Or God who is eternal light and blazing fire? Or the eternal faithfulness of the God of covenant love? There are great continents unexplored.

With God, there is always more; the eternal adventure has only just begun.

Thank you, my Father, that you have set eternity in my heart. Nothing finite can satisfy – only you can settle this restless heart. I praise you that in Christ and by your loving Spirit, you make yourself known to me, answering my longing for you and sharpening my longing for the day when we will be face to face. May I know you better and so love you more, that I may live for your glory forever.

Amen

Starting the Journey

Heaven is more full of joy over you than you could possibly know!
Look at Luke 15, verse 5 and verse 20 and see the Father's delight in
welcoming you home.

Does this mean that life will now be perfect and that you will
instantly stop sinning? Sadly, not until heaven! But you now have a
Saviour who is quick to forgive and who will change you day by day to
be more like him. You never have to face the challenges of life alone.

When we try to go it alone, it all goes wrong. Satan whispers
accusations and doubts into our minds. Thankfully, God gives us:

- The power of his Holy Spirit and prayer.
- The Bible, God's living word. Start with the New Testament
  books of Luke and John and get to know Jesus.
- The church, where God meets us, through baptism and
  communion, through worship and prayer and community
  and so much more.

If you are yet to find a church, please contact me at kate@
giftofblessingtrust.org so that I can pray for you, send some resources
and connect you with others. If you want to explore further, both
www.alpha.org and www.christianityexplored.org are helpful
and I recommend the resource page on Canon J.John's website
https://canonjjohn.com/how-to-become-a-christian/.

*For God so loved the world that he gave his one and only Son, that
whoever believes in him shall not perish but have eternal life.*

JOHN 3:16

Endnotes

1 John Henry Newman in Mary Tilestone, ed., *Great Souls at Prayer* (James Bowden, 1899).

2 'He has made everything beautiful in its time. He has also set eternity in the human heart; yet no one can fathom what God has done from beginning to end.'

3 Robert Llewelyn, ed., *Enfolded in Love, Daily Readings with Julian of Norwich* (Darton, Longman & Todd, 2004), p32.

4 CS Lewis, *The Last Battle* (HarperCollins, 2009).

5 Albert C. Outler ed., Augustine, *Confessions and Enchiridion* (SCM), p31.

6 George Eldon Ladd is illuminating on the present and future aspects of the kingdom of God in his book, *The Theology of the New Testament* (The Lutterworth Press, 1977, revised 1991).

7 Samuel Rutherford in Andrew Bonar, ed., *Letters of Samuel Rutherford* (Banner of Truth, 1664/2012), Letter XXVI, pp83–84.

8 Kate Patterson, 'Chasing the Wind' (2016).

9 'Markus Persson: the Minecraft billionaire sending lonely late-night tweets from Ibiza', *The Guardian,* 1 September 2015.

10 CS Lewis, *Mere Christianity* (Collins, 1952).

11 John Donne, 'Thou hast made me, and shall thy work decay?' in *Holy Sonnets*

12 Quoted by John Stott, *The Message of Romans BST* (IVP, 1994)

13 One example would be Matthew 11:21–24. This book cannot begin to cover the topics of eschatology and judgement in full but I hope that it will prompt you to take time to study the Scriptures on this and read around it.

14 Tom Wright, *Surprised by Hope* (SPCK, 2007), p150.

15 Miroslav Volf gives a helpful global perspective on the judgement of God in his book, *Exclusion & Embrace: A Theological Exploration of Identity, Otherness, and Reconciliation* (Abingdon Press, Revised 2019).

16 Simon Ponsonby, *And the Lamb Wins: Why the End of the World Is Really Good News* (David C Cook, 2008), p251.

17 From the hymn, 'Come, ye Disconsolate' by Thomas Moore.

18 Corrie Ten Boom, *Each New Day* (Fleming H. Revell, 1977).

19 Billy Graham, *Hope for Each Day* (Harper Collins, 2014).

20 Augustine, Sermons, trans. Edmund Hill, in *The Works of Saint Augustine: A Translation for the 21st Century,* ed. John E. Rotelle, Part 3, Vols. 1–11 (New City Press, 1992). (My emphasis.)

21 www.opendoorsuk.org/act/letter/iranian-prisoners/.

22 Quoted in Stephen Seamands, *Give Them Christ: Preaching His Incarnation, Crucifixion, Resurrection* (IVP, 2012), p49.

23 Revd Dr Michael Lloyd, GodPod 5, 'Resurrection and New Creation', sptc.htb. org/taxonomy/term/369.

24 CS Lewis, *The Voyage of the Dawn Treader* (HarperCollins, 2002), p18.

25 NT Wright, *Surprised by Hope* (SPCK, 2011), p226.

26 Gordon Fee, *Paul's Letter to the Philippians* (Eerdmans, 1995), p331.

27 Bede, *A History of the English Church and People*, translated by Leo Shirley-Price, ed R.E.Latham (Penguin, 1968).

28 Leon Morris, *The Gospel According to John*, (Eerdmans, 1995) p637.

29 Kate Patterson, 'The Wall' (unpublished, 2017).

30 Andrew Murray, *The Holiest of All* (Oliphants, London), p266.

31 Elfrida's story is told in my first book, Kate Patterson, *Promise of Blessing* (Muddy Pearl, 2015). For more of the story of God's work in Hong Kong, you can read Jackie Pullinger, *Chasing the Dragon* (Hodder & Stoughton, 2006).

32 Leon Morris, *The Gospel According to John* (Eerdmans, 1995), p637.

33 Craig.S. Keener, *The Gospel of John, A Commentary,* Vol. 1 (Hendrickson, 2003) p424.

34 Andrew Murray, *Devotional* (Whitaker, 2006), p83.

35 John Henry Newman, 'God is All in All' in *Prayers, Verses and Devotions* (Ignatius Press, 2019).

36 Mary Kissell, *Before the Days Draw In: My Ordinary Journey Towards an Extraordinary God* (Instant Apostle, 2018).

37 *The Journal of John Wesley*, ed., Percy Livingstone Parker (Moody, 1965), p419.

38 Vanessa LoBue, 'Violent Media and Aggressive Behaviour in Children' in *Psychology Today* (January 2018).

39 Mary Oliver 'Where Does the Temple Begin, Where Does It End' in *Devotions* (Penguin Random House, 2017).

40 Gerard Manley Hopkins, 'God's Grandeur' in *Poems of Gerard Manley Hopkins* (Humphrey Milford, 1918).

41 Annie Dillard, *Pilgrim at Tinker's Creek* (Harper Row, 1974), p7.

42 Ibid, p9.

43 CS Lewis, *Reflections on the Psalms* (Geoffrey Bles, 1958).

44 Andrew Murray, *The Holiest of All, An exposition of the Epistle to the Hebrews*, (Oliphants, 1969).

45 Jonathan Edwards, *The Works of Jonathan Edwards,* Vol. 2 (Banner of Truth, 1974), p909.

46 Charles Haddon Spurgeon, *Till He Come, Addresses at Metropolitan Tabernacle* (Christian Focus, 1970).

47 Charles Haddon Spurgeon, *Morning and Evening* (Crossway, 2003), Evening Devotional, 24 February.

48 Curran and Hill, 'Perfectionism is increasing over time: A meta-analysis of birth cohort differences from 1989 to 2016. *Psychological Bulletin,* 145 (4) 410-429 https://psycnet.apa.org/ (accessed 21 August 2020).

49 Moltmann, *The Trinity and the Kingdom of God* (SCM, 1981), p42.

50 Geerhardus Vos, 'Jeremiah's Plaint and Its Answer,' in Richard B. Gaffin Jr., ed., *Redemptive History and Biblical Interpretation: Shorter Writings of Geerhardus Vos* (Presbyterian & Reformed Publishing, 2001), p495. With thanks to the Toll Lege website where I found this quote.

51 Kenneth Bailey, *Jesus Through Middle Eastern Eyes* (SPCK, 2008), p99.

52 Luigi Gioia, *Say it to God: In Search of Prayer, The Archbishop of Canterbury's Lent Book 2018* (Bloomsbury Continuum, 2017), p51.

53 Kenneth Bailey, ibid.

54 Henri Nouwen, *The Return of the Prodigal Son* (Darton, Longman and Todd, 1994), p103.

55 Heidi Baker, *Compelled by Love* (Charisma House, 2008).

56 The final line of this prayer is based on Connor Patterson's song 'Adopted'.

57 William Joseph Seymour, quoted by Howard Peskett and Vinoth Ramachandra, *The Message of Mission, BST* (IVP, 2003), p216.

58 Songwriters: Christopher Joel Brown, Cody Carnes, Kari Brooke Jobe, Steven Furtick; The Blessing lyrics © Sony/ATV Music Publishing LLC, Universal Music Publishing Group.

59 This prayer is often attributed to St Francis but its first appearance was in France in 1912, probably written by a Catholic priest for his congregation. It was timely as it circulated widely in the two world wars that followed soon after.

60 James L. Mays, *Psalms: Interpretation: A Bible Commentary for Teaching and Preaching* (Westminster John Knox Press, 1994), p116.

61 Kenneth Bailey, *The Good Shepherd* (SPCK, 2015).

62 By way of comparison, the recommended maximum safe weight to lift at work is 25 kgs, or 55lbs, which is also the weight limit for luggage on an aircraft or the weight the British Army Infantry carry in their packs. This lost sheep is between twice and four times that limit!

63 Charles H. Spurgeon, 'The Parable of the Lost Sheep,' in *The Metropolitan Tabernacle Pulpit Sermons,* Vol. 30 (Passmore & Alabaster, 1884), 30: 526.

64 Mark Sayers, *Reappearing Church* (Moody Press, 2019), p139.

65 John Newton, 'Letter XVI – November 5, 1774', *The Works of John Newton* (Hamilton, Adams & Co., 1824), p494.

66 John Newton, 'Amazing Grace' in Cowper and Newton, *The Olney Hymns* (1779).

67 Sebastian Haffner, *Defying Hitler: A Memoir* (Orion, 2002).

68 John Goldingay, *Daniel,* Word Biblical Commentary, (Zondervan, 1987).

69 Niall Ferguson, *Empire: How Britain Made the Modern World* (Penguin, 2018).

70 Bill Neely, 'Berlin Wall's Fall was Greatest News Story I Ever Covered' *NBC News*, 9 November 2014, nbcnews.com (accessed 13 August 2020).

71 Percy Shelley, 'Ozymandias' in *Poems* (Everyman's Library, 1993).

72 Brueggemann, *The Prophetic Imagination* (Augsburg Fortress, 2001), p65.

73 https://www.message.org.uk/history/.

74 Ibid.

75 Rankin Wilbourne *Union With Christ: The Way to Know and Enjoy God* (Gospel Light, 2020).

76 B Westcott, *The Gospel According to St.John: Authorized Version with Introduction and Notes* (John Murray, 1896), p20.

77 Fleming Rutledge, *The Crucifixion : Understanding the Death of Jesus Christ* (Eerdmans, 2017), p244.

78 Ibid.

79 GB Caird, *The Revelation of St John the Divine* (A&C Black, 1966).

80 Andrew Murray, *The Holiest of All* (Lowe and Brydon, 1960) p310.

81 I first came across this quote in the challenging book by Jamin Goggin and Kyle Strobel, *The Way of the Dragon or the Way of the Lamb* (Nelson, 2017).

82 Fleming Rutledge, *The Crucifixion: Understanding the Death of Jesus Christ* p247.

83 Rowan Williams, *God With Us: The meaning of the Cross and Resurrection – Then and now* (SPCK, 2017), p45.

84 Jürgen Moltmann, *The Trinity and the Kingdom of God* (SCM, 1981), p36.

85 See Richard Bauckham for helpful thoughts on this in *Jesus and the God of Israel: God Crucified and Other Studies on the New Testament's Christology of Divine Identity* (Paternoster, 2008), p46.

86 Tom Holland, 'Why I was wrong about Christianity' *NewStatesman*, 14 September 2016, newstatesman.com (accessed 13 August 2020).

87 Simon Ponsonby, *And the Lamb Wins: Why the End of the World Is Really Good News*, p57.

88 Stephen Fowl beautifully describes it as 'cruciform' in *Philippians: A Two Horizons Commentary* (Eerdmans, 2005).

89 Kate Patterson (2019).

90 Lincoln Harvey, 'God in Action: Re-imagining Baptism', *Franciscan*, September 2016, franciscans.org.uk (accessed 16 August 2020).

91 CS Lewis, *Prayer: Letters to Malcolm: Chiefly on Prayer* (Geoffrey Bles, 1964), p92.

92 John Wimber, speaking live, Anaheim Vineyard, 1984.

93 Jerry Sittser, *A Grace Disguised: How the Soul Grows through Loss* (Zondervan, 2004).

94 Dallas Willard, *The Divine Conspiracy: Rediscovering our hidden life in God* (Harper Collins, 2014).

95 George Herbert, 'Artillerie', *The Complete Poetry* (Penguin Classics, 2015).

96 Miroslav Volf, *Free of Charge: Giving and Forgiving in a Culture Stripped of Grace*, (Zondervan, 2005).

97 Some readers will be aware that, tragically, one of the prominent leaders who followed Bash was involved in secretly abusing several boys. The perpetrator, John Smyth, died in 2018, after the case came to light but before he was convicted. He had been Chairman of the Trust which ran the Iwerne camps some years after Bash left. The camps were run in an overly authoritarian fashion and, sadly, this probably contributed to the slowness in bringing Smyth to justice. Archbishop Justin, along with the others mentioned here, knew nothing about this abuse until the allegations came to light and has expressed deep sadness about it. But Bishop Andrew Watson, who has bravely admitted to being one of those who suffered, is clear that what happened was not related to the expression of evangelical faith espoused at Iwerne, '*Abusers espouse all theologies and none; and absolutely nothing that happened in the Smyth shed was the natural fruit of any Christian theology that I've come across before or since. It was abuse perpetrated by a misguided, manipulative and dangerous man, tragically playing on the longing of his young victims to live godly lives.*'

gift of blessing trust

If you would like receive regular inspirational input from Kate, then you can connect with her at www.giftofblessingtrust.org. There you can find talks by Kate as well as "The Wisdom of the Elders" page which contains interviews with wise Christians from the older generation. You can also find Kate on Facebook at her Gift of Blessing Trust page, www.facebook.com/blessingkatepatterson

The vision of Gift of Blessing Trust is the vision behind this book - to root lives deeply in the love of God, for everlasting fruit. God wants each of us to thrive and bear fruit, even in this broken world of storms and droughts. It is here that we are to make a difference that will impact eternity.

We deeply believe that God has a part for you to play that no-one else can and our hope is that the Trust will help make that happen, connecting us together to support one another in this wonderful journey of knowing the God of forever.

*I pray that you, being **rooted and established in love**, may have power, together with all the saints, to take hold of how wide and long and high and deep is the love of Christ... that you may be filled to the measure of all the fullness of God.*

EPHESIANS 3:17–19